Experience and Faith

Experience and Faith

The Significance of Luther for Understanding Today's Experiential Religion

WILLIAM HORDERN

AUGSBURG Publishing House • Minneapolis

EXPERIENCE AND FAITH

For Nancy

Contents

Preface

During the past decade most church members in the United States and Canada have heard a great deal about a variety of religious experiences. Some of these experiences such as speaking in tongues or the born-again experience have been around a long time. In the last decade, however, they have become more popular and have occurred frequently in denominations where formerly they seldom appeared. Other experiences, such as the various forms of Eastern mysticism, are relatively new to our culture. All of these experiences have forced Christians to ask about the place of experience in the Christian life.

Many Christians have been troubled by the new emphasis on experiences. If they have not had some of these experiences, does that mean that they are not Christian? Are there different grades of Christians, depending on the amount and nature of experiences? Should we ardently seek experiences that we have not had or should we patiently wait for the Holy Spirit to act? Questions like these have troubled individual Christians and also split congregations.

This book does not attempt to give a series of techniques to handle experiential differences among Christians. It attempts to understand the place of experience in Christian faith. It is written for pastors who have to minister to people who are concerned about these questions and for the laity who wish to understand their faith more adequately.

Many persons helped in the writing of this book and I cannot here thank all of them. I do thank the Board of Governors of Lutheran Theological Seminary, Saskatoon, for the sabbatical that gave me the necessary time. As always in my writing, I am grateful to my wife, Marjorie, for her careful reading of the manuscript and many helpful suggestions. She continually helps me to speak to the problems of the laity in a language that is not overloaded with technical jargon. It was a pleasure this time to have both of my sons, Richard and Davis, read the manuscript and to make their cogent suggestions. Finally, I am grateful to Laurie Houston for typing the manuscript.

I An Age of Experience

EXPERIENCE HAS BEEN A DOMINANT THEME in North American religion since the early nineteen seventies. This is evident when we look at the publication of religious books in this period. Books dealing with various forms of experiential religion have been much more numerous and more popular than books of a theological or philosophical nature.

Parish pastors report that many church members claim that their religious experiences have led them to see the falseness or superficiality of the doctrines and practices of their churches. Congregations have been split when some members have achieved an experience that other members did not share and often did not appreciate. It was not unusual for those who had the new experience to claim that only those who shared it with them were really Christian. The mainline denominations have been abandoned by many members who became convinced that these denominations did not offer the opportunity and stimulus for the ecstatic experience that could be found in other groups.

The seventies were a time when the charismatic movement, emphasizing among other things the experience of speaking in tongues, was on the upsurge. Transcending Protestant denominational lines, even transcending the Roman Catholic-Protestant division, charismatics found a fellowship built on a common experience rather than on doctrinal agreement. Charismatic conventions have drawn crowds that are amazing both for the numbers involved and for the ecumenical nature of the participants.

In 1976 Jimmy Carter's campaign for the presidency of the United States brought the concept of "born again" Christians to the attention of the news media. In the election campaign of 1980 all three major candidates described themselves as born again. Although it may have taken presidential campaigns to get the news media interested in the born again experience, it had been making its presence felt in North American life long before Jimmy Carter made the news.

During the seventies the born again movement began publishing "Yellow Pages" which listed businesses that were operated by born again Christians. The implication was that born again Christians should give preference to the businesses that were so listed. This implicit boycott of non-born again business persons was not simply a concern to Jews, Muslims or atheists. It was equally a concern to the Christians in the major North American denominations for the term, "born again Christian" has come to mean a person who has undergone a particular form of religious experience. People might be ardent and practicing Presbyterians, Roman Catholics or Lutherans, but if such Christians cannot point to a time and place where they have undergone an ecstatic experience of conversion then, by definition, they are not "born again."

The shift to religious experience in the seventies brought about a change in the attitudes of students coming into theological seminaries. In the sixties many of the seminary students were dedicated to the battle for social justice. This dedication led them to be highly critical of the institutional Church and its ways. A large portion of the graduates opted for some vocation other than the traditional ministries of the churches. In the seventies the people who came to the seminaries were more concerned with their inner spiritual development than with social concerns. They sought this inner development both through traditional methods of piety and through the new psychological-sensitivity practices that gained popularity in the seventies. They criticized their seminaries for a lack of emphasis on "Spiritual Formation." These seminarians sought ordination in such numbers that several denominations had an oversupply of ministers. The people of the churches breathed a sigh of relief since it appeared that seminarians were no longer out to bury or remodel the church.

But this relief on the part of the churches was premature. The students of the sixties and early seventies were loud in their criticism of the church but this criticism arose from out of an underlying love for the church and a belief that the church was capable of doing great things. Their highly vocal criticism arose from this combination of love and hope. They condemned the church for its failure to redeem society in the way in which they believed it was capable of doing. They had a real hope that their criticisms would stir the church into action. But many of the students of the later seventies had no great love for the church and certainly no great expectations about what it could achieve. Therefore, they had no reason to criticize it for not being what they never expected it to be. For them the church, at best, offered a place where they could meet like-minded persons with whom to cultivate the inner life of experience. Churches, they assumed, were large organizations with programs and bureaucracies and as such could not contribute much to the inner life. That is best done in smaller groups of the like-minded. And so, in practice, these students have revived the old concept of the true church as a small vital group within the larger lethargic membership.

The religious movement of the seventies often has expressed

suspicion of any disciplined study of the Bible or theological analysis. It believes that the truth of religion comes through experience, not by conceptual analysis. This is why it is incorrect to refer to this movement, as many have done, as a "new evangelicalism" or even a revival of fundamentalism. There are a few parallels between this new movement and the older fundamentalism. Both, for example, have affirmed the inerrancy of the Bible and opposed historical methods of studying it. But the differences are greater than the parallels. Fundamentalism was always a rational movement, dedicated to a rigorously logical analysis to vindicate the truth of what it understood as historic Christianity. The contemporary movement is mostly indifferent to doctrine, which explains the ecumenical flavor in "charismatic" gatherings today.

This new movement in religion emphasizes experience as both an end in itself of the Christian life and as a means to discover the truth. This kind of emphasis is not an isolated phenomenon in Christian circles, on the contrary, it is the Christian manifestation of a much wider trend in our culture. The seventies were often called the "Me Decade" because it was a time when a great many people turned to themselves to cultivate their inner lives. This has been manifested in non-Christian religious ways through the continuing interest in Eastern religions and through the semi-religious Transcendental Meditation. It was also manifested in nonreligious ways by the popularity of various forms of psychological aids to inner development. Best-selling books have provided a variety of ways in which to find inner peace, happiness, and self-confidence. Various groups have flourished on the promise of helping people to get to know and accept themselves.

Behind the trend to develop the inner life there are a variety of sources. But it is interesting to see that one of the sources of this trend is the counterculture movement of the sixties. At first this movement was primarily a social and political protest against the "establishment" and the reigning culture. In the sixties it was optimistic about the possibilities of changing and improving society. Students hoped that they could bring about a revolutionary change in society by starting with their own educational institutions. Demonstrators against racial discrimination fully believed the words of their marching song, "We Shall Overcome." There was a widespread conviction that world poverty could be abolished as the Green Revolution and expanding technology solved the problems of scarcity. Even when the Vietnam War darkened the horizon, it was believed that a firm stand by the young would bring it to a hasty end. The concept of "participatory democracy" gave rise to a hope that the alienation between governors and the governed was soon to be overcome.

These high hopes of the sixties came crashing down in face of the facts of the decade. By 1969 historian Martin Marty could report that many of those who in the early sixties were offering Utopia "now envisioned Armageddon, the realm of conflict, final battle, and the end, as the only possibility."[1] There were many reasons for this loss of optimism. The youthful generation that set out to right inherited wrongs had seen the assassination of the Kennedy brothers, and Martin Luther King, three men who incarnated the ideals and style upon which much of the counterculture was based. Students had been gunned down in cold blood at Jackson State and Kent State universities and society seemed to have condoned it. The war in Vietnam went on unaffected by the protests. Riots in the cities had resulted in more misery for the oppressed minorities. The youthful revolutionaries were beginning to realize that the establishment had too many battalions on its side.

The rapid decline from optimism to pessimism is illustrated by two quotations from William Hamilton, a theologian who has always had a keen eye for the changing mood of the times. In 1966 Hamilton could argue that the reason the neoorthodox theology had lost it former dominant position was that "pessimism doesn't persuade any more." [2] But in 1970 Hamilton could write that the young people could not be persuaded by Jurgen Molt-mann's *Theology of Hope* because they knew that, in this apoc-alyptic age, "There is no historical future to hope in or for." [3]

When the counterculture moved from optimism to pessimism, it also moved from political action to inward personal develop-ment. A transition from the one to the other is found in Charles Reich's best-selling book, *The Greening of America,* which ap-peared in 1970. This book was still highly optimistic about the new future that was to be achieved but Reich did not see political action as the means to achieve it. It was to come by the conversion of individuals to the new consciousness of the counterculture. As he put it, "To fight the machine is to experience powerlessness. To change one's life is to recapture the truth that only individuals and individual lives are real. . . . We must answer the doubters by saying that their methods have failed and failed and failed, and that only changing one's own life confronts the real enemy." [4] Spokespersons for the new left attacked Reich as a "revolutionary ostrich", and called his book a "cop out" but he was correct in foreseeing that the counterculture would turn from social action to the individual self. However, Reich's optimism about the social effects of personal conversion were lost as the counterculture turned inward and made the individual's development an end in itself. In the later seventies several of the revolutionaries of the sixties reappeared as apostles of inward experience, in some cases they appeared as born again Christians.

A major outcome of the counterculture was a loss of faith in science, reason and technology. Ever since the Enlightenment, the Western World, particularly North America, had defined progress in terms of the advance of reason, science, and tech-nology. This trinity was hailed for having cured disease, ban-ished superstitious fears and produced an abundance of material goods and services to enhance the standard of living. Of course, there were always critics of science and technology, but such critics were on the fringes of society and could be dismissed with amused contempt as fanatics or "know nothings." What happened in the counterculture was that resistance to the scientific-technological culture appeared among the middle class youth who had been reared in technological luxury and trained in the universities.

Two of the books that were popular in the counterculture were *The Technological Society* by Jacques Ellul and *One-Dimensional Man* by Herbert Marcuse.[5] Ellul argued that the quantitative growth of techniques had resulted in a qualitative change that resulted in what he called the "technological society." Whereas originally techniques had been used as means to achieve human purposes, in the technological society techniques became the ends themselves. Instead of serving human needs, the technological society forces human beings to adapt to the demands of technology. Technological efficiency rather than human need becomes the dominant factor. As a result human beings find themselves living unnatural lives, divorced from their home in nature, packed into polluted cities, working at uncreative jobs. True humanity always involves an element of spontaneity and unpredictability but the technological society has to have routine and predictability to operate and so education in the technological society becomes propaganda to make the human being like a machine—unspontaneous and predictable. The technological society rests on two basic premises: the chief end of human beings is to attain happiness and happiness is achieved through an increased abundance of material comforts and luxuries. Given those two premises, the only questions left are the ones about technological efficiency. But Ellul's picture of humanity caught up in the demands of technology raised a serious doubt about the second of these premises, a doubt that appealed to the counterculture.

Herbert Marcuse charged that our rational technological society has resulted in a "one-dimensional" person. That is, it has encouraged us to see all of reality in terms of the one dimension of those things that can be seen, weighed and measured. As someone has summed it up, "If you cannot see it, feel it, taste it, hear it, smell it or if you cannot kill someone with it or make a profit out of it, then it does not exist." In this society, Marcuse charged, people have become enslaved because they have been captivated by false needs. Marcuse called his readers to break out of the one-dimensional existence and to realize the depths of reality that have been lost through the net of the scientific-technological view of reality.

A prominent spokesman for the counterculture, Theodore Roszak, pointed out how the counterculture differed from the old radicalism. The old radicalism never questioned the capitalistic view of the importance and value of scientific technology. Its concern was to distribute the fruits of technology more equitably. "It was not foreseen even by gifted social critics that the impersonal, large-scale social processes to which technological progress gives rise—in economics, in politics, in education, in every aspect of life—generate their own characteristic problems." [6] And so the counterculture was a revolt, says Roszak, against the alienation involved in the scientific-technological world view.

Roszak goes on to describe how scientific knowledge is rooted in the search for power. Scientific knowledge gives power, it creates an elite group that has control over the masses because it has the knowledge to keep the technological machine running. And so Roszak calls his readers to an experiential search for truth that eludes the scientific dimension of life. In the process, he is highly critical of religion as it has developed in the Western World. Christianity has become a religion of the word instead of a religion of experience. He charges that a religion which becomes concerned with belief and doctrine is "the last fitful

flicker of the divine fire before it sinks into darkness." [7] In Roszak
we see the counterculture's disillusionment with all that reason
and science had accomplished and the truths they could discover.
In a bitter passage, Roszak says, "Before the earth could become
an industrial garbage can it had first to become a research laboratory." [8]

Having become disillusioned with the rational-scientific-tech-
nological world view, the counterculture was open to other ways
of knowing. It embraced Eastern mystical religions, dabbled in
magic, and exalted inner experience as a road to deeper truths.
The counterculture explored the use of various drugs to enhance
its inner experience. In part, of course, the use of illegal drugs
was a way of protesting against the establishment. The technological society produced a drug culture, as we might expect
if Ellul's charges were true that technology forces humans into
an inhuman way of behavior. The drugs of the technological
society have been legalized—alcohol, caffeine, tranquilizers, sleep-
ing pills, pep pills, etc. The counterculture's use of illegal drugs
was a protest against the establishment's practice. But there was
more. To many in the counterculture it seemed that their minds
had been so conditioned by the presuppositions of the technological age that they could not truly see reality. They needed the
mind expansion that chemicals could induce so that they could
break through their conditioning and see reality in a new way.
There was always, therefore, a religious element in the drug culture which explains the popularity of the writings of Carlos
Castaneda.

The opposition of the counterculture to rational-scientific ways
of thinking led naturally to a development of inner experience.
As the disillusionment about reforming society grew, this development of inner experience became more and more an end in
itself. This helps to explain why the revolutionaries of the sixties
could reappear as the mystics or born again Christians of the

seventies. It may seem a long way from the counterculture to born again Christianity and yet there was one group in which the transition was apparent—the so-called "Jesus People" of the early nineteen seventies. Many of the early Jesus people came from the counterculture and even used much of the counterculture language, particularly that of the drug culture, to describe their Christian experience. They termed themselves "Jesus freaks" and talked of "taking a trip" on Jesus instead of on LSD. Quite rapidly the Jesus movement was taken over by the established churches and absorbed into traditional patterns, but the themes of finding truth in inner experience rather than through reason and science were continued. Charismatic experience, particularly speaking in tongues, seemed to be an especially appealing way of breaking from the controlled and predictable ways of reason, science, and technology.

Despite the link that the Jesus movement provides between the counterculture and born again Christianity, it is not my thesis that the two movements are intimately connected. My point is that later development of the counterculture and experiential forms of Christianity are both part of a wider trend of our culture toward a development of the inner life's experience.

The counterculture's journey into inner experience is, in many ways, untypical of the journeys taken by others to similar destinations. The counterculture was naturally literate and it attempted to interpret and justify its behavior. But many, and perhaps most, of those who have turned inward have not thought of it as a revolt against the reigning world view of our time. For these people, it has been a natural response to their situation in life. As we look through history we find that in every age marked by change and insecurity, there has been a turn to inner experience. The decade of the seventies was one in which a whole culture was exposed to change and insecurity.

Our Western society has experienced (and is still experiencing)

an era of almost unparalleled change. As the decade of the
seventies opened, someone remarked that anyone over thirty was
an immigrant to the nineteen seventies. This was a profound
comment. Immigrants live in a culture different from that in
which they have been raised and trained to think and act. For
a long time we have recognized that an immigrant is subject to
"culture shock," a psychological reaction to the drastic change in
culture. But the rapid changes of our time mean that people can
stay in the same geographical location and yet find that they are
immigrants in the culture. Hence the term "future shock" was
coined to describe the problems involved in living in a time of
rapid change. [9] A person can handle only a limited amount of
change within a given period, even if the changes are desirable.
Alvin Tofler gives considerable medical evidence to justify his
statement, "Future shock is the dizzying disorientation brought
on by the premature arrival of the future. It may well be the most
important disease of tomorrow." [10] Certainly change has been
coming at us rapidly. People who were born and raised in the
horse and buggy era lived to sit in their living rooms and watch
television while men walked on the moon. But change is not
limited to the technological realm. Moral values that were once
unquestioned have become dubious or have been abandoned. The
plaintive plea for a return to "traditional" or "biblical" values
expresses the sense of disorientation that comes from living in
a world where one's views of right and wrong are no longer
axioms accepted by all. Social values likewise have changed.
Within the space of a few years we have seen culture move from
the extended family to the nuclear family and finally to the place
where the family itself is under question. The roles of male and
female are in flux and creating confusion for many. The work
ethic, concepts of success, and a basis for a sense of self-worth
are all undergoing change.

We have said that there is a limit to how much change can

be handled in a given period even when the change is desirable, but many of the changes being faced today are far from welcome to the people undergoing them. As Ellul points out, our technological society has worked on the premise that happiness, the goal of life, is to be achieved through the acquirement of more and more of the physical comforts and luxuries of life. Suddenly the Western World has been forced to face the fact that there are limits to growth in our "space ship earth." Much of our prosperity has been built on cheap energy but, with the rapid depletion of the hydrocarbon fossil fuels, and the militancy of the OPEC states, we are facing the fact that the era of cheap energy is past. Our economies are locked into what is often called "stagflation." Economic theory used to say that inflation and unemployment do not happen together, but in stagflation, they do happen together. Prices are going up because our standard of living is being forced down and, as various power groups try to protect themselves from this inevitable decline, there is more money to buy fewer goods. Very slowly it is creeping into our consciousness that the human race cannot be supported in the manner to which North Americans have become accustomed. We have lived for a long time in the faith that things would always get better, growth would continue to bring higher standards of living for all. But the time has come when we have to face the fact that probably never again will we have it so good. Instead of assuming that today's children will have greater wealth than we have had, we have to face the fact that they may well not have the standard of living that their parents have enjoyed. These are hard facts for our society to face and so a spirit of frustration and fear is abroad. The violence that occurred in the line-up at gasoline filling stations is a vivid example of this frustration.

There are many other elements of insecurity that could be mentioned. In the democratic nations there has been a loss of faith in governments. In the United States this is especially related to

Watergate, but in other Western countries, such as Canada, there is also a lack of confidence in governments even where there has been no such scandal. The threat of thermonuclear or bacteriological warfare remains in people's minds. This fear surfaces in the battles over the development of nuclear power that have occurred in most of the industrially advanced nations.

When the external world becomes a source of change and insecurity, it is natural that people turn inwards. As we have said, through history, in all times of major social change and periods of insecurity, there has been a widespread cultivation of the inner spiritual life. As we shall see in a later chapter, this occurred at the time of the Reformation. When "Change and decay in all around we see" it is inevitable that many will look inward for that which changes not. In a sense of being related to God, the self, or the universe, a person finds a supporting rock in the midst of a world of change. Much of the revival of experiential religion in our time is, therefore, a natural reaction to the change and insecurity through which we are passing.

It helps in understanding the current emphasis on inner religious experience when we see it as a response to the change and insecurity of our times. But it does not help to evaluate it. Some, of course, would argue that what we have in this phenomenon is a failure of nerve and an escape from the real problems of the external world to the safe irrelevancies of inner life. And, no doubt, for some that is what is involved in the turn to inner experience. But others will argue that times of change and insecurity serve to reveal to us our idolatrous dependence upon the things of this transient world and thus open our eyes to the really real, and the truly true. And, no doubt, for some that is what is involved.

What is attempted in the following pages is to examine the place of experience in religion. In particular, we are concerned to ask what contribution it can make to religious knowledge. At a time when many people within the church are looking critically at the doctrines, practices and forms of their churches in light of their inner experience, it is necessary to ask to what degree such experience can be a criteria for doctrine and life. Furthermore, we shall be concerned to see what is the legitimate role of experience in the life of the Christian. Are there dangers in an emphasis upon experience? How does one evaluate experience? A very obvious aspect of experience is that it is used to justify opposing religious positions. When that happens, how do we judge between the conflicting claims? As we have noted, experience often becomes a divisive force within a congregation. Those members of a congregation who have a particular experience often claim that only those who have this experience are Christian. On the other hand, those who have not had the experience in question are sometimes prone to consider that those who have had it are some kind of freaks or are psychologically unbalanced. How does a congregation evaluate such claims and counter-claims?

To wrestle with these questions, we shall next spend a chapter on philosophical and theological considerations about religious experience, with particular reference to epistemological questions as to how experience gives knowledge. Then in three chapters we shall examine Luther as a case study in dealing with religious experience. Because the Reformation had many parallels to the current scene with regard to religious experience, Luther's comments take on a high degree of relevance for our times. In the next two chapters we examine concepts of experience that have arisen in the various liberation and political theologies of today. Here experience has quite a different meaning from what it usually has in the term "religious experience" but it is a view of experience that can throw light on the place of experience in theology. Finally, we shall try to draw some conclusions.

Experience, Knowledge, and Religious Experience

II

THE ROLE OF EXPERIENCE IN RELIGIOUS KNOWLEDGE has received much attention in theology for the last two centuries. Early in the nineteenth century, the philosopher-theologian, Friedrich Schleiermacher attempted to justify religion to its "cultured despisers." The cultured despisers were the intellectuals of his time who thought that they had outgrown religion because they could no longer believe the doctrines of the church and they had refuted the philosophical arguments for God's existence. But, affirmed Schleiermacher, "If you have only given attention to these dogmas and opinions, therefore, you do not yet know religion itself, and what you despise is not it." [1] True religion, said Schleiermacher, is never a matter of believing doctrines; it is experience, in particular the experience of feeling dependent upon the universe. Schleiermacher tried to show the despisers of religion that, although they had cast aside the trappings of religion, they were nonetheless deeply aware of the experience that is at the heart of all religion. The same theme was continued about a century later in Rudolf Otto who identified the basis of religion in the experience of the "numinous"—the sense of awe, wonder, and fascination that overwhelms people in certain situations. [2]

Liberal theology, following Schleiermacher, emphasized experience as the basis of religion and religious knowledge. It opposed all authoritarianism in religion and argued that nothing should be believed simply on the basis of authority. We should accept only those beliefs that are verified by our reason and experience. In a scientific age, liberals felt that no other basis of religion could be credible. They spoke of theology as an "empirical science."

Liberal theology always included a wide variety of opinions, as would be expected in a theology that rejected all authoritarianism. As a result, the nature of religious experience varied from liberal to liberal. In writers like Rufus Jones, experience referred to special experiences of a "mystical" nature that held their own authority for the person who had experienced them. But for other liberals, such as H.N. Wieman, experience referred to the whole of a person's experience in life and he paid little attention to experiences that could be set apart as "religious."

Neoorthodox theology, arising in the 1920s through the work of Karl Barth, set itself against the liberal emphasis on experience. Liberalism, charged the neoorthodox, had tried to go from humanity to God but the God of the Bible always takes the initiative so that knowledge comes from God to human beings. Liberal theology, in the tradition of Schleiermacher, charged Barth, could never escape the critique of Ludwig Feuerbach.

Feuerbach, in his book *The Essence of Christianity,* argued that all theology is really anthropology. That is, although theologians believe that they are talking about an objectively real God, in fact, they are simply speaking about themselves. God is humanity written large, a projection of human nature onto a heavenly screen. As Barth sees it, the attempt to know God through one's own experience is always vulnerable to Feuerbach's analysis. When theologians look into themselves for the knowledge of

God, Barth believes, they find a god created in their own image. Because human beings are self-centered, when they seek God, they naturally find the god they want to find. A theology based on experience has no defence against this kind of idolatry, says Barth.

Neoorthodoxy did not banish experience. It affirmed that all knowledge of God is dependent on God's revelation but it did not identify the Word of God with the words of Scripture. It is possible to read the Bible without hearing God speak. The words of Scripture become the Word of God when the reader is illuminated by the Holy Spirit. This obviously opens up possibilities of experience. But the experience is always related to the objective revelation by which it can be evaluated and in light of which it is understood. God's mighty acts in history, particularly the life, death and resurrection of Jesus, form an objective revelation that stands over against the subjectivities of experience.

We can better understand the issues involved in this theological debate on the place of experience if we take a brief look at some of the philosophical implications of experience with respect to knowledge. Empiricist philosophers have argued that all knowledge comes from experience. Without experience the human mind is a *tabula rasa,* a blank blackboard with nothing written on it. Empiricism developed as a refutation of those philosophies that had argued that people are born with some innate or a priori truths that are self-evident to the human mind. For example, in a famous passage Plato describes how Socrates asks questions of an untrained slave boy and proves, to his satisfaction, that the slave boy has an innate knowledge of certain mathematical theorems. Unfortunately, some of us who struggled through mathematics did not find such evidence in our experience. Some philosophers have argued that humans are born with innate ideas of what is right and wrong behavior but the wide diversity of moral codes casts doubt on this. Furthermore, anyone who has raised a child is fully aware that morality is something that has to be taught. We cannot simply let our children do what comes naturally to their inborn sensitivities. Over against all theories of innate ideas, empiricists insist that there is no human knowledge until we experience the objective world.

I do not intend to become involved in the debate as to whether all knowledge comes through experience or whether humans do have some inborn, innate or a priori knowledge. Suffice it to say that the burden of proof today is with those who would argue for an innate knowledge prior to experience. One of the unique aspects of human life is that, compared to other forms of life, humans are born with much less instinctual programming. The ant and bee, for example, have built into their gene structure a whole behavioral program which means that through centuries the social structure of the anthills and beehives have remained the same. But each human generation has to learn anew the wisdom of the ages. It is sometimes remarked that we are never more than one generation from barbarism. That is, each human generation has to be taught the ways of civilization anew. As a result, human social structures have varied greatly over the centuries. Without raising too many philosophical debates, therefore, we can say that obviously most and perhaps all human knowledge arises from out of experience.

But, having said this, we still have the problem of what do we mean by "experience?" First, we mean what comes to us through our five senses. No one would deny that a vast amount of what we know comes as a result of seeing, feeling, tasting, hearing and smelling. But there is a major philosophical debate as to whether or not these five senses are the exclusive experiential source of knowledge. Many empiricist philosophers and all positivistic ones would argue that our five senses are the sole basis for human knowledge. However, there is a long-standing philosophical tradition which has argued for experience that is not dependent upon any of these five senses. Mystics have talked of a "sixth sense" or the "eyes of faith" or "the inner light" to describe an experience of God which brings its own knowledge independently of the five other senses.

If we take a "common sense" view of experience, it would seem that all of us are aware of experiences that are not, in any simple way, related to the five basic senses. Most people would say that they have experiences of love, hate, sadness, joy, frustration, satisfaction, worry, peace and a host of others. Such experiences are never divorced from the experience of the five senses but they do have an independence of their own. For example, I receive a letter from a friend which I have to touch and see in order to read. But as I read it I experience joy, sorrow, anger etc. dependent upon its message. These feelings do not come without the experience of the five senses, but when they come they have an independence from them. Another person reading the same letter would not have the same experiences. In another time and place I might have different experiences as I read the same letter. In short, a person's awareness of life is not limited to what is seen, felt, smelt, heard, or tasted; it also includes the fact that life consists of experiences of love, joy, sorrow, hope, despair and so on.

Positivist philosophers or behavioristic psychologists refuse to grant the term "knowledge" to what they consider to be the "private experiences" or "emotions" such as joy, sorrow, pain and love. They argue that before they can provide knowledge, such private experiences must be translated into terms that can be verified publicly. This means that they must be expressed in terms that can be detected by one or more of the five senses. Thus, if I want to say that George is feeling sad, I have to be able to point to some publicly observable act. I must say that I mean George is crying or beating his brow or something of that nature. But, in actual personal relationships, we are frequently fully justified in saying that we know George to be sad even when we cannot detect any publicly observable sign of it. (After all, George may be noted for keeping a "stiff upper lip.") Of course, such claims to knowledge are fallible, as are all human claims to knowledge. Our five senses deceive us. In the same way, we may be sure that George is sad because we would be sad in George's situation but we are mistaken because George is different from us. But if we allowed fallibility to rule against speaking of knowledge, we could never say that we know anything.

Another challenge to the claim that all knowledge comes through the five senses arises with the claims of extrasensory perception. Many intelligent and scientifically minded people are prepared to argue the case for extrasensory perception. They can point to some highly significant experiments where certain "psychic" persons have read unseen cards or received unheard messages with an accuracy that defies the laws of chance. But, from the scientific point of view, such experiments are frustrating. Scientists like experiments that can be reduplicated ad infinitum. But the person who can correctly identify unseen cards at a rate well above chance today may totally fail the same test on another occasion.

The whole field of extrasensory perception is highly controversial and open to many conflicting points of view. Therefore, it might seem best to ignore it in a discussion of religious experience and most discussions do ignore it. But it cannot be passed so quickly. The mystics who claim to possess a sixth sense or an eye of faith may not like to be classified with mind readers or psychics but they do have much in common. Both groups claim to gain direct knowledge through a form of experience that is independent of any of the five usual senses of human beings. If mental telepathy were to be proven beyond reasonable doubt, it would certainly force us to consider the possibility that the mystic is able to communicate directly with the mind of God.

When we define experience in terms of the data of our five

senses plus our inner feelings and perhaps even extrasensory perception, it becomes evident that most knowledge comes to us from experience. And so, it would seem obvious that if we are to have religious knowledge, we must have religious experience of some kind. Does it not seem, therefore, that those who emphasize the priority of religious experience over theology or other aspects of the religious life are simply pointing to the obvious?

But the problem is not solved that simply. All knowledge may presuppose experience but the relationship between experience and knowledge is complex. For example, I have the experience of seeing an object and I say, "This is a bridge." My knowledge that it is a bridge, however, does not come simply from my experience of seeing it. If I have someone with me who is learning the English language, this person does not see a "bridge." To know that is a bridge, I must know the English language. But it is more than just that. To know that this is a bridge, I have to have seen other bridges. Perhaps this object does not look like any other bridges that I have seen, but I note that it stretches from one bank of a river to the other and people or vehicles could cross over it. And thus I reason from past experience and decide that this object, even if it does not look like one, is a bridge. Without going into a further analysis, it is evident that our knowledge based on experience is a complicated matter that involves what has been learned in the past, memories, and inevitably a considerable amount of reasoning to draw conclusions.

For our purposes, this is important. When people say that they have experienced God, we need to be rightfully skeptical. What do they mean by "God?" Obviously, in the world there are many different meanings of the word, "God." When we hear that someone has experienced God, we have to ask, "Which God?" The experience alone cannot answer this question. It is a well known fact that the writings of the mystics around the world seem to be describing similar experiences. But when the mystics speak of the God whom they have experienced, they describe God in terms of their particular culture and tradition. The experience, important as it no doubt is to the mystic, seldom reveals a new God.

This means that we cannot eliminate theology and have experience pure and simple. The experience always has to be interpreted and when we interpret it we are doing theology. It may be good, well thought out theology or it may be slipshod uncritical theology. From a purely philosophical approach we can see that experience without interpretation (i.e. theology) is meaningless. The person who claims to be living by experience alone, without theology, is really sneaking in a particular theology. There is a biblical basis also for this conclusion. John calls us to test the spirits. (1 John 4:1-3) That is, John is warning us that our experience of the divine has to be examined. Not every experience of a spirit is an experience of the Holy Spirit. The testing of the spirits is a theological task so the New Testament joins the philosophical analysis in calling for theological interpretation.

Because experience needs to be interpreted and tested, we need to take a look at how experience is used. I can illustrate my point by a reference to the natural sciences. These sciences are called empirical sciences because they are based on experience. All scientific knowledge is based on what scientists have experienced. Experiments have to be observed, dials have to be read etc. in order to construct hypotheses. If scientists had no experiences, there would be no science. But when we read a textbook on science, we do not read about scientists having experiences, we read about experiments and so on. All that the scientist learns in a laboratory is based on experience but scientists do not study their own experiences, they study the physical world. They do not call attention to themselves but to the world outside of themselves.

This analogy is relevant to the religious scene. All parties may agree that our religious knowledge is based upon experience but that leaves considerable room for difference as to how experience is treated. Those who exalt religious experience often tend to concentrate on themselves and their feelings. Theology for them becomes a matter of analyzing how they feel in what they think of as religious situations. Those who are suspicious of the current emphasis on religious experience want to emphasize that we ought to seek knowledge of God, not of our experience. Our aim should be to find out what God is doing, not how we are feeling.

This is brought out by Roger Nostbakken in a paper on the charismatic movement. Having read extensively in the literature of the charismatic movement, he comments,

> One realizes after having read many of the testimonials that one has learned a great deal about the persons but very little about the Spirit or Christ. The focus is inescapably anthropocentric, one is constantly amazed at personal transformation, and is happy for them but somehow the glory does not seem to belong to God. One marvels at the person rather than God. [3]

Nostbakken has noted a phenomenon that is often found where religion emphasizes experience. On the one hand, the language used by the advocates of this viewpoint abounds in references to God, Christ, Spirit, grace, and so on. And yet we often end up with the feeling that the person is pointing to himself or herself. *They* have achieved the goal of experiencing God, Christ, and the Spirit. A recent popular evangelistic campaign flooded us with slogans announcing, "I Found It." The impression inevitably arises that the finders have somehow acted so that they have been able to experience what others have missed.

This is illustrated in the work of Larry Christenson, a charismatic Lutheran pastor. Christenson makes an effort to interpret speaking in tongues within the framework of the traditional Christian view of the priority of God's grace. Even so, we find Christenson saying, "The initial hurdle to speaking in tongues, it seems, is simply this realization that *you* must 'speak forth.'

(Many people wait and wait for something to 'happen,' not realizing that the Holy Spirit is waiting for them to speak out in faith!)"[4] In short, where religious experience becomes the center of attention, it is easy to fall into a works-righteousness in which one gets those experiences of God which are earned or deserved.

It is like having a textbook in science which consists primarily of autobiographies of scientists. Autobiographies of scientists have their place but they do not do a great deal to inform us about the physical world. Similarly, religious autobiographies have their place in the life of the church but by themselves they cannot give us a reliable knowledge about God. As Karl Barth saw, this approach to theology is defenceless against the charge of Feuerbach that theology is anthropology, its god is but human experience projected onto the heavens.

The point we are making is illustrated in the life and thought of a Christian leader who is often appealed to by the exponents of religious experience. John Wesley, in launching his historic revival, called people to experience the religion that they had long professed in theory. Important in Wesley's life was his so-called "Aldersgate experience." At a time of personal searching, Wesley walked into the meeting house at Aldersgate while a selection from Luther's commentary on Romans was being read. As he listened, Wesley reports that his "heart was strangely warmed." This event has become a symbolic event for followers of Wesley and its importance has been magnified beyond what historical facts can warrant. It was not Wesley's conversion, it was not even his call to ministry. Nonetheless, it did give him a new vision, motivation, and direction in life. However, where this event has been emphasized, it has often had the result that followers of Wesley tend to go around taking the temperature of their hearts. They continually examine themselves to see if their hearts are properly warmed because this is their primary test of whether they are in the right relationship with God. But this overlooks the fact that when Wesley's heart was "strangely warmed," Wesley was not looking at his own heart, his attention was drawn from outside of himself toward God's act in Christ as that was being presented through the words of Martin Luther.

Wesley never made the mistake of supposing that experience, his own or any one elses, could become the final authority of truth in Christian faith. Wesley believed and preached that Christianity is a living personal relationship to God and where this relationship is not experienced, Christian faith is incomplete. Nonetheless, Wesley was careful to distinguish between such experience and authority for belief. As Colin Williams demonstrates, "It is true that only by the inward witness of the Spirit we can understand the meaning of true faith in Christ, but the Spirit brings this understanding to us through the Church's witness to Christ. Experience therefore is the appropriation of authority, not the source of authority."[5] Wesley was aware that religious experiences vary widely from each other and so "in Wesley experience is not the test of truth, but truth the test of experience."[6]

The point we are making is that to concentrate on our own experience is to give only information about how we feel. This has its interest and importance. But it cannot be claimed that it gives knowledge of a reality apart from ourselves. Experience contributes to knowledge when the experience is centered on that which is apart from ourselves. This principle, obvious in the physical sciences or common-sense approach to reality, is also valid in the case of religious experience. To know God it is not sufficient to examine how we feel, we need to look outside of ourselves to where God is manifest apart from our inner experience. Granted that we cannot know God without experience, nonetheless knowing God is knowing more than how we feel.

So far in this discussion we have not defined what we mean

by "religious experience." The first definition that usually comes to mind is that of some special and unusually ecstatic feeling, feelings to which the term "mystical" might be applied. In short, religious experiences are outside of the ordinary experiences of life. In depth, intensity or in some such special quality, they stand out from the experiences of everyday life. They are "mountaintop experiences," or periods of ecstasy.

A serious problem in defining religious experience in terms of unusual or ecstatic forms of experience is that we have difficulty in distinguishing between an experience and a person's expression of that experience. It is a well-known fact that some people tend to give exuberant expression to their experiences while other people give little or no outward expression. One couple in love may manifest their love in many public expressions of it while another couple may make no public demonstration of their love. It does not follow from this that the first couple has a deeper or richer experience of love. One person suffering grief may weep and demonstrate in public while another person may show no outward signs of emotion. It is a serious mistake to conclude, as is so often done, that the second person is experiencing any less grief and sorrow than the first. The differences in expression arises from out of personality traits, environmental training and so on.

When we turn to religion, there is no reason to expect that the situation will be different. Two people with the same inner experience may express their feelings in radically different ways. I knew an elderly lady who belonged to a charismatic denomination. It remained a great sorrow to her that she had never "gone under the power" and spoken in tongues. She was certain that she lacked faith and underwent considerable anguish because of it. And yet, knowing her and her family, it was evident that this woman was not of a demonstrative nature. She had been brought up to keep her emotions under cover. We have no reason to suppose that she did not have the same experiences as those who spoke in tongues, but such an expression of them would have been quite out of character for her.

This observation is supported by a study of persons who speak in tongues that was made by a psychotherapist, John Kildahl, and a psychiatrist, Paul Qualben, who found that persons who spoke in tongues usually shared particular psychological traits.[7] It appears that those who do not have these traits are unlikely to speak in tongues. This bears out the view that because people express their feelings in different ways, it is misleading to limit the definition of "religious experience" to the more dramatic expressions of experience.

There is another problem in defining as religious certain unusual experiences. That is the problem of what distinguishes some unusual experiences as religious over against other unusual experiences which are not so defined. In recent years many people have argued that various drugs can be used to bring about religious experience. Some drugs do bring about, in some people, a sense of mind expansion, a clearer insight into reality and awareness of things formerly unnoticed. But why should we think of such experiences as religious? Why is the experience arising from taking LSD or mescaline a religious experience while we seldom hear it claimed that the experience one has after a third cocktail is a religious one?

For other persons, the very fact that drugs have been used would prove that the experience cannot have been a religious one. Where an experience has been induced by the introduction of chemical substances into the system, these people argue that the chemical and not God is the cause of the experience. The drug-takers are hence not experiencing God or the truth but hallucinations. The problem, however, is that experiences considered to be religious often occur in the context of a highly emotional religious gathering and this leaves open the suspicion that they may be caused by group suggestion or even hypnotism. Many of the mystics have taught extensive disciplines to bring about mystical experience and this raises the question as to whether the experience is caused by autosuggestion or self-hypnosis. If the use of drugs in themselves rules out an experience from being religious, do not these other external causes rule out the experiences occurring in their context?

A suspicion of illusion does not invalidate the claim that something was a "religious experience." There are illusory or false religions and so there can be illusory or false religious experiences. The basic question still is why some experiences of an unusual nature are called religious and others are not.

Under a variety of influences many people have what appear to be the same or, at least, very similar experiences. Some of these people describe the experience as religious and others do not. A few years ago the news media carried a story of a college where there was an outbreak of "speaking in tongues." All of the appearances indicated that here was an experience similar to that common in charismatic religious groups. But, in this case, it was emphasized that there was nothing religious about the experiences. It was a group-stimulated release of emotions, a psychological lift without any theological or religious implications. What makes one person's speaking in tongues a crucial religious experience whereas another person's similar experience is nothing but psychological release?

This same problem appears over a much wider spectrum. Most people who have religious faith have had particularly meaningful experiences, high moments in their lives. Perhaps these have come in a deeply moving church service or perhaps they have come in the presence of some beautiful natural scene or while viewing a painting or listening to music. In these moments the religious person feels close to God, is assured of God's reality and that God's will toward them is made manifest. But when the religious person tries to describe this to a nonreligious friend, the answer often comes back something like this: "Oh yes, I have had that same experience in similar circumstances. Such experiences mean a great deal to me but I have never thought of them as religious. I thought of them as aesthetic experiences." Once more we have the question of what makes the experience religious to one person and not religious to another?

Of course, a simple way out of this dilemma is for the religious person to say that the two experiences are obviously not the same. When I was moved to the depths of my being while viewing the grandeur of the mountain, I was in communion with God, its creator. The unbeliever, moved to the depths of his or her being in the presence of the same mountain was not in communion with God. Therefore, the experience was not the same for both of us. The difficulty with this line of approach is that we have no objective way of distinguishing a religious from a nonreligious experience. Insofar as it is possible to describe an experience to another person, it appears that the two experiences are identical. The two people felt the same way. But one of the persons wants to say that this is communing with God whereas the other does not want to say that. Of course, in the last analysis, all of our experiences are private. I cannot really know whether an apple tastes the same to you as it tastes to me. Much less can I know if my religious experience in the presence of a beautiful object is the same experience as the aesthetic experience of another person in presence of the same object. If I try to say that my experience is different because I experience God, I cannot verify this unless I can somehow point to God apart from my experience. All that we can say with assurance is that we define our experiences differently. Does this mean that a religious experience is made religious by the interpretation of the person who experiences it?

At first sight this may seem to leave us adrift upon a sea of relativity. But this does not necessarily follow. There is a respectable tradition that would define a religious experience as any experience of a person who is religious. The point of this argument is twofold. In the first place, it affirms that there are no particular experiences that come labelled as "religious." An experience becomes religious when the person who has the experience understands it as having religious significance. In the second place, it affirms that religious experiences are not simply a matter of a few "mountaintop" experiences or feelings of an unusual nature (although religious experience could include these) but it affirms that any experience or feeling can become religious when seen within the context of a religious faith.

Paul called upon us to pray continuously (1 Thess. 5:17). Given our normal definitions of prayer, that is an obvious impossibility. Normally we define prayer in terms of consciously speaking to God. We divide prayers into such categories as intercession, thanksgiving, praise, and confession but common to all of these types of prayer is that they are highly verbalized. Even if we go into our closet alone to pray in silence, we do not think that we are really praying unless we are forming verbal messages in our minds. In short, prayer consists of talking to God and listening for God to speak to us. Given such an understanding of prayer, it would be impossible to live a normal life and at the same time be continuously in prayer. How could we carry on a sensible conversation with the people around us and still be talking to God at the same time? How could we concentrate upon the various tasks we have to perform while continuing to talk to God? Did Paul really mean that we were to pray continuously or was this just a pious overstatement? That is, by urging people to pray continuously, was Paul really just urging them to pray more frequently?

Perhaps our problem with Paul's admonition to pray continuously is that we have defined prayer in a way that is too restricted. Let us define prayer as being in communication with God. Of course, speaking to God or listening for God to speak to us is then prayer, for speaking is a vital part of communicating. If, however, we examine our communication with other people, we find that often there is a deep communication without any verbalizing. In fact, our deepest communications with some persons often occur at a level beyond what words can express. When, for example, we wish to communicate our sympathy to someone who is experiencing tragedy, words often seem totally inadequate. Instead of speaking we put our arms around the person, weep with them, and in other nonverbal ways communicate to them more than we could say. Or again we may have a deep sense of communication with a good friend or loved one while simply sitting in the same room without speaking or doing anything. At other times we have a sense of communication with another person while together we are engaged in the same activities of work or play even though no words are spoken.

Paul seems to see analogies to these nonverbal forms of interpersonal communication and our communication with God. For example, he says, "Likewise the Spirit helps us in our weakness; for we do not know how to pray as we ought, but the Spirit himself intercedes for us with signs too deep for words" (Rom. 8:26). If this is so, then we can see that God may speak to us most clearly in and through the events of our daily lives. To pray continuously, therefore, does not mean a continual verbalizing to God, it means understanding the whole of our life in the context of our relationship to God. We see God's will and action in all our experiences. In short, every experience of the person with religious faith has the potential of being a religious experience. This is to pray continuously.

When we understand religious experience in this way, it follows that experiences which normally would be regarded as "secular" are now seen as being potentially religious experiences.

A religious dimension may come through working, playing, eating, and the like. We are still free to say that some of our experiences stand out from the rest in terms of significance for our religious life. Paul, who called for continuous prayer, certainly saw a particular significance in his Damascus Road experience. But it does not follow that such outstanding experiences will of necessity be in the context of so-called religious events. Our experience of God's presence may be deeper and more real at the birth of our child or in our relationship with a loved one than it is during a worship service.

When we think of religious experience in terms of any experience of a person who is religious, it throws a new light on the problem that we discussed earlier where two persons seem to have the same experience but for one it is religious and for the other it is not. Now we can concede that, for example, in the presence of an awe-inspiring natural setting, two persons have the same basic feeling or experience. The reason that it is religious for one person and not for the other is not to be found in any quality of the experience in one or the other person. What makes it religious for the one person is that this person, from out of religious faith, interprets it in a religious framework and thereby is brought nearer to God in and through the experience. The other person interprets the same experience in a nonreligious framework and sees no need to bring God into the interpretation. There is an interesting example of this principle in John's Gospel. Jesus, coming to Jerusalem for the last time and already beginning to wrestle with the temptations that peaked in Gethsemane, hears a voice from heaven speaking to him. The crowd standing around was divided upon what happened. Some said that it had thundered, some said that an angel had spoken (John 12:27-30). All present presumably had had the same experience but what it meant to each depended upon the framework within which he/she interpreted it. The same principle is implied in

Jesus' words, "He who has ears to hear, let him hear" (Matt. 11:15). The experience of hearing takes on meaning only as the hearer interprets what is heard.

The fact that the same experience may be interpreted differently does not abandon us to an inevitable relativity. On the contrary, it is a point of contact between persons. This is what Schleiermacher attempted to do with the "cultured despisers of religion" to whom he spoke. He first tried to find a common experience of believers and unbelievers and then he tried to persuade the unbelievers to interpret their experience in a new light. This attempt at apologetics needs to be handled carefully. We see this illustrated in the work of Paul Tillich. Tillich believed that believers and unbelievers share a common experience which he called being ultimately concerned. And so Tillich tried to show that even an atheist was really religious because atheists too are ultimately concerned. Many unbelievers were scandalized, however, and charged that Tillich had "baptized them by definition." We are not trying to argue that unbelievers really are religious although they do not know it. On the contrary, we are saying that religion arises as people consciously interpret their experiences in a religious way. A common experience shared by believers and unbelievers does not, therefore, mean that both are religious, but it does mean that they have a common point for discussion. They can attempt to persuade the other to reinterpret the experience in question.

When we define a religious experience in terms of the interpretation of any experience by a religious person, it becomes obvious that the term "religious experience" is too broad to be useful. No one has a religious experience in general, people have Christian experiences or Buddhist experiences or experiences of some other particular religion. That is, if it is the interpretation of an experience that makes it religious, the interpretation is not of religion in general but of a specific religion. In experience the Hindu believer is related to Brahma and loses the self in the great all-encompassing Self of Brahma. In experience the Christian believer is related in an I-thou way to the God of Jesus Christ. It is legitimate to speak of both of these as religious experiences inasmuch as a religion gives the basis of interpretation in both cases. But the uniqueness arising from the different interpretations must not be forgotten. We have no reason to believe that there are unique experiences associated with any particular religion. What differentiates between experience in one religion over against another is not to be found in the quality of the experience in itself but rather in the interpretation that is made of it.

If experiences become religious because of their interpretations, it is obvious that people do not gain theological ideas simply from their experiences. On the contrary, the experiences are usually interpreted in the light of theological ideas that are already at hand. Of course experience plays an important part in knowing. A person may have been taught a system of theological ideas and may believe them, but such belief may be merely a top-of-the-head acceptance. But the day may come when such a person has an experience in depth through which the beliefs already held become more vivid, real and decisive for the person. In short, there is a great difference between knowing something because we have been told about it and knowing the same thing because we have experienced it for ourselves. Nonetheless, the experiential knowledge depends for its interpretation upon what was believed or learned earlier.

Defining religious experiences as any experience of a person who is religious does not put raw experience as a final criterion of truth. On the contrary, it recognizes that all experience is evaluated and interpreted before it becomes a basis of belief or knowledge. Truth is much more complicated than having a strong feeling or conviction about something. Reason is never divorced from experience but reason must always be operative if experience is to be understood and interpreted so that it results in knowledge.

The point that we are making can be illustrated well in the death of God theology. The God is dead movement peaked in popularity during the year of 1965-66. Since that time, it is often quipped that The God is dead theology was a creation of the news media. This is not strange. According to the old adage, it is not news if a dog bites a man, but it is news if a man bites a dog. Similarly, it is not news if a theologian says that God is alive, but it is news if a theologian says that God is dead. As a result, the little circle of God is dead theologians experienced a few heady months when they were on the front pages of newspapers, hosted on radio and television and in great demand on college campuses. In 1966 TIME magazine's Easter issue had a black cover upon which was written in blood red letters, "GOD IS DEAD." The feature article dealt with the God is dead theology. This can be considered the peak of the popularity of the movement.

What the news media creates, it can destroy. When a man bites a dog, it is news but if a man goes out every morning and bites another dog, it soon ceases to be news. The media grew tired of theologians saying that God is dead and passed on to other matters. In 1967 William Hamilton, a leading exponent of the God is dead theology, had a short article in the *Christian Century,* titled, "A Funny Thing Happened on the Way to the Library." He pointed out that "radical theology," a term he always preferred to describe his work, had gotten waylaid by its popularity in the news media. In the process, it became apparent that the news media is no place for serious theology and so it was back to the library and some good hard work. [8]

When the God is dead theology disappeared from the news media most church people breathed a sigh of relief and assumed that once again God had been vindicated. But the movement did not disappear. It lived on particularly in the departments or schools of religion in secular colleges and universities. As a movement, it illustrates well the importance of interpretation to religious experience.

The term, "death of God" was inspired by the writing of the philosopher, Friedrich Nietzsche. The God is dead theologians used it, as an apt description of what they saw as a widespread experience of our century. It described the experience of those for whom once God had seemed real and present but who now find that they no longer experience God as real or significant for their lives. This experience comes not so much as a sense of a grievous loss but as a liberation. And, it has not meant that they have ceased to look to Jesus as the Lord in their lives. In 1974, Hamilton summed it up,

> Radical Theology tries to suggest that having had and losing is a specific sort of religious experience; it is not "loss of faith," and it differs from never having had, or from always having had. And some, but not all, of us are committed to the idea that the experience may be a Christian one. [9]

Hamilton analyses the term "death of God" by contrasting it to other terms used in mystical forms of religion, such as "eclipse of God," "Absence of God," "silence of God," and "disappearance of God." That is, the great mystics recognized that the experience of the believer involves a dialectic of possession and nonpossession. If there are the times when God's presence seems real and certain, there are other times when God is not experienced at all, God seems absent or nonexistent. It is to this family of terms that death of God belongs, affirms Hamilton. What then is the difference? Hamilton's answer makes it clear that it is a matter of how the experience is interpreted.

When the mystics spoke of the eclipse, silence or absence of

God, the terms were chosen to express an element of hope. Eclipses pass and the sun shines again, silent persons can speak up again and absent persons can return. And so the mystical language interprets the experience as a temporary time of trial and testing and looks forward to its reversal. But, says Hamilton, to use the term "death of God" is to express no hope or expectation of a speedy or predictable return. Hamilton is careful not to pontificate about the future and does not insist that God will never return to his experience. All that can be said is that the present experience has been one that leaves no reason for waiting and hoping for God's return. Life can be rich, full and meaningful for the radical theologian without God. Whereas the mystic went through the dark night of the soul when God was no longer experienced, the radical theologian goes on with the fascinating and exciting task of living in the world and seeking to find and serve Jesus in the events of this time and place. As Hamilton points out, the experiences of the mystics and the death of God theologians appear very similar. What is different is the interpretation. This illustrates our point that religious experience depends on the interpretation made of experience.

At the height of the popularity of the death of God theology, evangelist Billy Graham was quoted as saying, "I know that God is not dead because I talked to him this morning." The disagreement between Graham and Hamilton illustrates the limitations and value of religious experience. In no logical way did Graham refute the God is dead arguments. The one man says "God is dead, because I have experienced his death," the other says, "he is alive because I have experienced his living." But whose experience should we accept? Whose experience most accurately describes reality? Those who find that Graham's interpretation fits their experience will naturally agree with Graham and those whose experience is illuminated by Hamilton's interpretation will agree with him. Do we, then, take a public opinion poll to see which group is in the majority? That would be interesting but would prove nothing. Perhaps the truth is revealed to the little flock and not to the majority.

There seems to be only two alternatives in such a situation. We can, like children in argument, shout at each other, "my experience is better than your experience," or we can attempt to analyse and interpret the experiences involved to see which is more valid. We can "test the spirits" and, while this will not win universal agreement, at least it will make possible a meaningful discussion between the two groups. In such a discussion each may come to a better understanding of his or her own experiences. For example, one of the important contributions of the God is dead theology is that it forced many Christians to take a new look at themselves. For, charged the God is dead theologians, many who claim to believe in God do not show any evidence for it in their lives. Their political decisions are made along the same lines as others in their social and economic class, their ethics are the basic morality of respectability of their time and place, the important decisions in their lives are made upon the same criteria as those of their unbelieving neighbors. What difference in their lives is involved in saying that they believe in God? What would be different if they ceased to believe in God? In fact, is not God really dead for such believers, even though for sentimental reasons they cling to belief? By being faced with such a challenge, many believers were forced to re-evaluate their faith position. In the process some came to a new appreciation of their faith and some decided that, in fact, God was dead for them. When we recognize that religious experience needs interpretation, it opens up such possibilities for fruitful evaluation of our experience.

If religious experience depends on interpretation, how do we go about interpreting it? In the next chapters we shall examine Martin Luther's thought as a historical case study in how experience may be interpreted within a Christian framework.

III Luther and Religious Experience

IF LUTHER WERE TO APPEAR on the North American scene today he would find himself very much at home with the contemporary emphasis on experience in religion. He faced similar trends and ideas in his own time. This is not surprising because there are many parallels between our time and the time of the Reformation. It too was a time of radical and rapid change as the old medieval order was breaking up. The Reformation itself was a challenge to the rule of the Catholic church that had lasted for over a thousand years. The economic order of feudalism was disintegrating and the new bourgeois-capitalistic system was beginning to appear. The power of the Holy Roman Empire was passing and the new national states were beginning to take form. There was social unrest, and revolution was in the air. On the international scene, the Muslims were a continual threat and Europeans feared at any moment to be overrun by what they saw as Godless hordes. The invention of the printing press had brought about a revolution in communications as great as radio and television have done in our time. It was a time when people felt threatened and were seeking for security. Many went on pilgrimages, bought indulgences and did a host of other works to gain an assurance of salvation. And, as today, a great many turned to the inner life to find the security that the outer world could not give.

It is somewhat misleading to speak of *the* Reformation because there were really four reformations or, at least, four wings of the Reformation. Although these four influenced each other, they were distinct from each other. In Europe there were both the Lutheran and the Reformed (Calvinistic) reformations and in England there was the Anglican reformation. On both the continent and in England there was a fourth reformation, variously designated as "Anabaptist" or "radical," or "sectarian" or "left wing." It is this fourth reformation which is most interesting from the point of view of religious experience.

The Anabaptist or Radical movement was not a unified or homogenous one. Within it there were far greater differences than within any of the other three wings of the Reformation. Modern descendants of this reformation such as Mennonites, Quakers and Baptists, have deplored the fact that, both at the time of the Reformation and in later history, the revolutionaries, fanatics and pacifists were all lumped together by their critics. Pacifists often paid with their lives for the actions committed by revolutionaries. Certainly, it was a major injustice of history that the important distinctions between these various groups were overlooked. Nonetheless, there are a number of common themes that ran through the various groups in the radical reformation which make it possible to speak of them as one of the wings of the Reformation. One of these common themes was the emphasis on religious experience.

A stimulating book by a Canadian Mennonite, Harry Loewen, has brought to our attention the significance of the radical reformers for the development of Luther's thought.[1] Loewen's thesis is that in many ways Luther's theological stance was clarified and developed by dialogue and debate with the Anabaptist groups. Generally speaking, most studies of Luther's thought have concentrated upon his debates with the Roman Catholic and Reformed traditions. But Loewen demonstrates that we cannot fully understand Luther's position until we see it also over against the radical reformers. And certainly it was in relation to these groups that Luther worked out his stand on religious experience.

Luther's relationship to the radical reformers is a complex one. Loewen compares it to King Lear's relationship to his daughters.[2] The analogy is apt because most of the radical reformers began as Luther's followers, they were his spiritual and intellectual children. But, as they drew Luther's ideas to what they believed were logical conclusions, they became in Luther's view rebellious children.

This tension-filled relationship between Luther and the radicals existed on many issues, Baptism, the Eucharist, liturgical practices, the use of art in the churches, and relationships to governments. But a central key to the tensions is to be found in the question of the place and role of experience in faith.

To begin with, it is important to see that Luther's experience was an important factor in bringing about the Reformation. Caught up in the general feeling of insecurity of his time, Luther searched for religious security and assurance. He wanted desperately to know that he was saved. After his traumatic experiences with the death of a friend and his own narrow escape from lightning, Luther took the most radical route to security available in his world. He entered a monastery and dedicated himself with zeal to all of the good religious works encouraged by the church of his time. Luther was so zealous that he confessed his sins daily until his bored confessor finally told him to go out and commit some sins worthy of confessing before he came back. But in all of this Luther failed to find a sense of peace or security.

Perhaps Luther had a guilt-complex and thus could not find the peace that he sought. In recent years many attempts have been made to locate such a complex by psychoanalyzing Luther. But, after the passing of so many centuries, the best that can be achieved through this means is merely speculation. We just do not have adequate information to make a persuasive analysis of Luther's psychological problems. If, however, we go by what Luther has said in his writings, we can conclude that he was ruthlessly honest with himself and with the scriptural message. Luther knew that even when he had done the most rigorous of good works, his motivation for doing them was self-centered. He was not acting because he loved God with all of his heart and mind and strength, he was acting because he wanted to save Martin Luther's eternal soul. He was serving God because it was good for himself. But, as Luther read the Scriptures, it became evident that they called for a quite different kind of righteousness. For example, Paul said, "If I give away all I have, and if I deliver my body to be burned, but have not love, I gain nothing" (1 Cor. 13:3). Paul's point, as Luther saw, is that even if one performs heroic acts of goodness such as giving away all possessions or dying a martyr's death, it is not the righteousness that God seeks unless it has been done for love. Jesus criticized those who gave to charity to establish a reputation for themselves (Matt. 6:2-3). Luther saw that so long as a person is serving God with the aim of benefitting the self, it is not the righteousness that God seeks.

Faced with this understanding of Scripture, Luther saw his own passionate search for salvation to be as selfish as that of a person who sells his or her soul to make a worldly fortune. This led Luther to despair. If we can please God by performing certain meritorious actions (good works), then by an effort of the will we can bring ourselves to do some amazing things. We can make sacrifices and perform incredible feats. But if God is interested not in *what* we do but in *why* we do it, then what can be done? By an effort of will, we can make ourselves do various things, but by no effort of the will can we make ourselves do them for the right motives. If we are acting from out of self interest, how can we remove our self from the center of our lives? If we are to change or improve our self, we must pay attention to it. But the more attention we give it, the more we become concerned with it. The Middle Ages, in its search for security, put considerable emphasis on self-denial—fasting, celibacy, poverty, etc. Surely such actions remove the self from the center. But, Luther saw, these too may be done to win something for the self. Often in the Middle Ages, it was emphasized that what was given up in the self-sacrifice was really worthless compared to the reward that was to be gained. And, as Luther saw, this gave the whole show away. The seeming acts of self-denial were really an affirmation of the self on a more subtle level.

And so Luther's study of Scripture forced him to see that he was helpless to build his own security. He was "curved in on himself" and any effort that he made to overcome this problem simply intensified his concern with himself. In short, his will was in bondage, he could do nothing to free himself from the shackles of egocentricity. He fell deeper and deeper into despair. His only hope was that something outside of him could liberate him from his bondage.

It was at this point that one day Luther read the words of Habakkuk, "But the righteous shall live by his faith" (Hab. 2:4) and as the Quakers would put it, they "spoke to his condition." The Bible took on a wholly new meaning for Luther. It was not a law, laying a demand upon him that he must fulfill to win God's favors, it was rather "gospel," good news.

The good news was that what Luther could not do for himself, God had already done for him in Jesus Christ. The doctrine of justification was seen to mean that God would accept him as he was. And at last Luther experienced the peace and sense of security for which he had searched so long. His peace and security were not based on anything he had done or was, they were based on what God had done and is. And because it was God's grace that had saved him, Luther could have the assurance that his own works could never have brought to him.

In a very real sense, therefore, the Reformation was born in Luther's experience, both his experience of failing to achieve peace and security by his own works and in his having found peace and security by relying upon God's acts. As Bengt R. Hoffman sums it up,

> Does God meet us in wrath or goodness, as death or life, through law or gospel? This became Luther's problem with the nature of God. This problem was resolved, insofar as it can be resolved in human existence, by the way in which Luther experienced God. [3]

It is not surprising, therefore, that it could appear that over against the pope, monasticism and the medieval church, Luther had set his own experience. In calling for the priesthood of all believers, Luther seemed to have called upon each person to find within himself or herself the reality of God that could not be given by the church, priests, sacraments or pope. In the early years of his reform, Luther often spoke in ways that would encourage such interpretations. The radical reformation emphasized this aspect of Luther's thought. We shall take a look at some of the radical reformers to see how they were related to Luther.

Thomas Munzer is known to history as a revolutionary, an instigator of the Peasants' Revolt. Marxian writers have found in him a kindred spirit and so we do not usually think of this man of action as one who was primarily concerned with inner experience. But, at the heart of Munzer's theology was the dream of a new church of the spirit that was to come. It would be a church that did not depend upon hierarchies, sacraments or the literal letter of the Bible. As Munzer put it in his "Prague Manifesto" "God inscribes with his finger in the hearts of men his immovable will and eternal wisdom." [4] For Munzer, the Bible is only a matter of paper and ink until God opens the mind of the reader, and this God does, giving assurance to people that they are children of God. In short, the Bible is inadequate without a divinely inspired interpreter of the Bible and Munzer was confident that the Holy Spirit was with him so that he was such an interpreter. On the other hand, he could say that anyone who had not received the personal experience of the living God would be unable to speak correctly about God even though such a one had eaten a hundred Bibles.

Munzer did not believe that this personal experience of God would come to a person without preparation. He taught a series of steps, including repentance of sin and reform of one's way of life whereby one could become sufficiently worthy so that the Holy Spirit would come with illumination and salvation. This represents a tendency, wide-spread in the radical reformation, to see experience of God as the fruit of a process of disciplined preparation on the part of the believer. As such, this links the radical reformers to those traditional forms of mysticism which have taught that the mystical experience of God comes only to those who have properly prepared themselves.

As time passed, Munzer's religious experience brought him the revelation that he was to be a new prophet of God, bringing in a new age. God was speaking to him and urging him to encourage the down-trodden peasants to revolt. With confidence he told his followers that they would not have to fight alone, God would be with them, causing their enemies to fall before them. In this pathetic hope, Munzer died in battle as the peasants were decisively defeated. In a similar way Jan Mathys felt called by the Holy Spirit to take over the city of Munster and set up a new society there. After a brief period of successful revolution, Mathys and his followers were ruthlessly killed by a combined army of Roman Catholics and Protestants.

Because Munzer and Mathys were led by their spirits to revolution, it was not difficult for Luther to defend his position and to distinguish himself from them. But other radical reformers were not so easy for Luther to handle. The so-called "Wittenberg Radicals," Carlstadt, Storch, and Stubner, all claimed to be true followers of Luther, carrying his ideas to their logical conclusions. In their minds, although Luther had set the church back on the road to truth, he was too timid. Hence they were in more of a hurry than Luther to reform the structures of the church, and began to go much further than Luther in repudiating its practices. They seem to have been the first of the Reformers to repudiate infant baptism, although they did not rebaptize those who had been baptized as infants as later radicals did. Like Munzer, they acted in the conviction that they were in direct communication with God and were fulfilling his directions. In a letter to Wittenberg, Luther warned the people against the teaching of these "enthusiasts" saying, "When these men talk of sweetness and of being transported to the third heaven, do not believe them. Divine majesty does not speak directly to men." [5] From these words it appears that the Wittenberg Radicals were claiming particular ecstatic religious experiences which gave them direct revelations from God.

As time passed other Anabaptist groups came to Luther's attention. Men like Hans Denck, Sebastian Franck, and Caspar

Schwenckfeld insisted that they were but following where Luther had led. As Luther had come to see in his experience the centrality of justification to the biblical message, they were allowing the Spirit to lead them into all truth, and so they put their primary emphasis on the inner light or experience of God that had illuminated them. Denck summarized the position when he said, "Scripture is a lamp unto our feet, but since it is written by men it cannot remove the darkness completely. Only Christ in the heart of the believer can remove all darkness." [6] Such views led the Anabaptists to see infant baptism as invalid. Water cannot bring salvation, only the gift of the Holy Spirit can do that. And so they taught that a person should not be baptized until after the Holy Spirit had been received. Hence the term "believer's baptism" was used to express the conviction that baptism was valid only when applied to one who already believed and had the Holy Spirit.

One of the problems in calling these groups "Anabaptist" is that the term gives the impression that baptism was a very important concept to them. Actually, it was not. Their faith was not of a sacramental variety. For them the important thing was the baptism of the Holy Spirit; that and that alone could save. When a person had been baptized by the Holy Spirit, it was also a good thing to be baptized by water, for Jesus commanded his followers to do so. But its purpose was not to bring salvation—the baptism of the Spirit already had brought that; its purpose was rather as a public witness to what God had done and could do for others.

This view of baptism meant that before a person could be baptized by water, the life of the person had to be examined to see whether, in fact, there was evidence of a baptism by the Holy Spirit. This meant that there had to be evidence of sanctification, that is a life increasingly lived in accordance with the teaching of Jesus. A major argument of the Anabaptists against infant baptism was that far too many people who had been baptized as infants showed no evidence in their lives of the work of the Holy Spirit. Infant baptism, therefore, was seen as dangerous because it had given such people a false sense of security. They believed that, in being baptized, they had been accepted by God and saved. Resting complacently on their baptism as infants, such people did not seek the baptism of the Spirit.

There are many obvious parallels between these views of the Reformation radicals and views that have been popular for the past decade. The concept of baptism by the Holy Spirit has been emphasized in the charismatic revival. Doubts about infant baptism have been expressed by many people even in those churches that have always practiced it.

We have talked about certain features that the radical wings of the Reformation shared, and here it is important to see a major difference within their circles. To Munzer and other revolutionaries, the kingdom of God was to be an external social order which would be brought in through the action of the saints. But Denck and Mennonite groups differed from the revolutionaries in that they saw the kingdom of God as a reality within the individual believer. As such the kingdom of God was identified with an inner experience of God. Of course, as already mentioned, they did believe that this inner dwelling of God within a person would result in outward actions in harmony with the teachings of Jesus.

The radical reformers who identified the kingdom with the inner experience naturally argued that outward or objective things cannot be of decisive importance. The important thing is what happens in the heart, for salvation is an inward process, initiated by God through the divine Word and through the Christ who dwells within. Thus, the Bible, water baptism, eating bread and wine at the Lord's Supper, the church as an institution and liturgical actions, all being external things are not of decisive importance. In fact, there was some tendency in these groups to so emphasize the Christ who dwells within that they tended to overlook Jesus, the man who lived in Nazareth. This was not an intention to bypass Jesus, it was just that they believed that Jesus came most vividly to them, not through the Gospel accounts of his life but in their internal religious experience. Having walked and talked with Jesus in their inner lives, it did not seem as vital to them to read about him in the pages of Scripture.

It is obvious that these exponents of religious experience could claim to be following where Luther had led. Luther's experience had led him to see in Scripture the centrality of justification and the law-gospel dichotomy. It is well known that Luther had a low opinion of certain portions of Scripture. Because he found little of the gospel or Christ in the book of James, for example, he could call it an epistle of straw and even said that he would use it to heat his stove. [7] How then could Luther complain when others used their religious experience to justify new doctrines on baptism, the Lord's Supper and so on? Luther had emphasized the priesthood of all believers. Did this not mean that each individual could look to his or her experience as the ultimate authority? Was not then Luther the spiritual father of all those radicals who followed where their experience of God led them?

It was face to face with these challenges that Luther was forced to refine his understanding of experience. We shall try to summarize the major points that Luther made to clarify his position over against the radicals. As we do so, it will become evident that this is not just an historical exercise. Luther has an important word to speak to the contemporary religious scene with its emphasis on experience.

The first point to see in Luther's response to the radicals is that, despite the importance of his experience, Luther never wavered in his doctrine of *sola scriptura*. That is, the Scriptures alone are to be the final authority. No matter how vivid or persuasive an experience of God may be, it must be tested by God's Word in the Scriptures.

Luther's doctrine of the Scripture was not simplistic. He did not see the Bible as an inerrant message in the sense that we could take any passage from Genesis to Revelation and preface it with "God says . . .".

At first it seems paradoxical that although Luther could emphasize the Scriptures alone, he could equally well speak of "Christ alone" or "grace alone" or "faith alone." We are tempted to protest against Luther's lack of logic here. After all, you cannot have more than one thing "alone." But Luther knew what he was saying. He was not trying to identify four different things but to say the same thing in four different ways, each way bringing a new insight into its meaning. Basically, Luther was committed to Christ alone. Christ is the primary Word of God (John 1:1-14). When God speaks and communicates with humanity, Christ is always the Word through whom God speaks. And so in creation, God's Word was the prime agent of creation (Gen. 1:3, 6, 9, 11, 14, 20, 24, 26; John 1:3). It was God's Word that came to the prophets of Judaism and enabled them to dare to preface their preaching with "thus says the Lord . . ." For Luther this meant that Christ, the Word, is not simply to be found in the New Testament; Christ permeates the whole of Scripture. And so, for Luther, God's communication with us is always "Christ alone." There is no other Word that God might speak. This Word of God became flesh in Jesus of Nazareth (John 1:14) and spoke most clearly to us but the incarnate Christ was the same Christ who had been with God in creation, who had illuminated the prophets of old and who, through the form of the Holy Spirit, would be eternally with the church.

The message spoken by Christ, the Word of God, is primarily the message of grace. Yes, the Word speaks the law, the commandments of God and the judgment of God, but the final word is always that of grace, of God's forgiving love that seeks and accepts God's erring children. Grace means that what we human beings could not do for ourselves, God has done for us in and through Christ. Because Christ's primary Word is always grace, it is not a contradiction to say both, "Christ alone" and "grace alone." It is but two ways of saying the same thing.

The grace offered to human beings in Christ is received simply and only through faith. Grace is not something that we earn or deserve, it is simply to be accepted by us trustfully. Whereas from the side of God in Christ it is grace alone, from the human side it is faith alone. And so again, to say "faith alone" is not to add paradoxically another to the list of things that are alone, it is once more to say the same thing differently.

But how is it that we Christians know Christ as the Word of God who speaks the word of grace to be accepted in faith? We know it because the Scriptures bring us the message. The Scriptures are, therefore, of prime importance because they bring to us the message of Christ. In an oft-quoted phrase, Luther spoke of the Bible as the "cradle" that contained Christ.[8] This is an apt way to summarize Luther's understanding of Scripture. For all of his emphasis upon the Scriptures as the authority to stand against the authority of the pope or the church, Luther did not see the Bible itself as something divine. The Bible was important because it brought to us the Christ.

When Luther spoke of the Scriptures alone, he did not imply that God is limited to the Scriptures. For example, in his preface to his commentary on the Book of Jonah Luther says,

We have here again an outstanding example of the thing St. Paul is talking about in Rom. 3:29 "Is God the God of the Jews only? Is he not the God of the Gentiles also? Yes, of the Gentiles also." This account shows that even this wicked kingdom of the Assyrians was a concern for God—although they were uncircumcised Gentiles not belonging to the people of Israel, whom God had chosen for himself. And what is more, they were oppressing Israel. Thus God always has had his Christian people among all nations along with the Jews, . . . So there is no doubt that there are here and there in the world today many Christians who are totally unknown to the world, whom God has chosen for himself. [9]

This passage makes it clear that Luther believed in the power of God through Christ to reach people outside of the Christian church. Unlike many Christians, Luther was convinced that the loving God revealed in Jesus Christ would find ways to win people even where there was no church to carry the message. When Luther spoke of the Scriptures alone, therefore, he was speaking from out of the context of the Christian church. God can find ways to speak to all people but God has chosen to speak in and through the revelation in Jesus Christ which is recorded for us in Scripture. Here God's Word speaks to us most simply and clearly. Once this revelation has been received, it is recognized as the primary revelation in light of which all other claims to revelation must be tested. For the Christian, therefore, the Scriptures are the final authority, they alone must be used to test doctrine and belief.

Luther was convinced that basically the Scriptures brought a simple message that any Christian could understand. One did not have to be a learned scholar to decipher Scripture, but this did not mean that the message of Scripture is understood without effort. Luther never assumed that a person could open the Bible at random and identify the first words read with God's words to us. The message of the Bible called for study and work upon the part of the reader. Luther did insist upon taking the "literal" meaning of Scripture. But the term "literal" had a much different connotation for Luther than it has today. For Luther it was contrasted to the wide-spread medieval custom of interpreting the Bible allegorically. Over against the fanciful ideas read into Scripture by the allegorists Luther insisted on taking the "literal" meaning. We would call it the "natural" meaning or even the "common sense" meaning.

For Luther, taking the literal meaning of the Bible did not mean that we can take any single biblical verse and use it as a proof text for our point of view. This is illustrated in Luther's reaction to Carlstadt and other radicals when they used biblical statements against idolatry to justify their destruction of statues and other art forms in the churches. Luther says, "It is not valid, however, to pick out one word and keep repeating it. One must consider the meaning of the whole text in its context." [10] This remains a basic principle in Luther's interpretation of Scripture: each passage must be understood in terms of its context.

But as one wrestles with a text of Scripture, it is evident that the context stretches out until it includes the whole of Scripture. Luther was sure that, because Christ comes to us throughout the Bible, we need to weigh each passage in light of the whole message of Scripture. There are times when Luther appears to be proof-texting his position. For example, we think of his famous debate with Zwingli when he seemed to rest his case on a simplistic affirmation of the verse, "This is my body" (1 Cor. 11:24). But as we study Luther's view of the Lord's Supper, it is obvious that he interpreted this verse within the total context of Scripture and in light of the Christ who had been present in creation, spoke through the prophets, became incarnate in Jesus and was now universally present through the Holy Spirit.

But to truly understand a passage of Scripture, Luther recognized that the context also includes the historical setting within which the passage was written. And so Luther says, for example, that to understand Isaiah

> It is necessary that one know how things were in the land, how matters lay, what was in the mind of the people—what plans they had with respect to their neighbors, friends, and enemies —and especially what attitude they took in their country toward God and toward the prophet. . . . [11]

Luther came to see the doctrine of justification as central through his experience. But he did not present his experience as the authority to oppose pope and church. Rather, he searched the Scriptures as a whole and was convinced that he could demonstrate that the Scriptures themselves bore out the centrality of justification. When he was critical of books or passages of Scripture, it was not because he set his own experience, illumination or revelation against these passages of Scripture; it was because he found that they were out of harmony with the main thrust of Scripture as a whole. They failed to speak a clear word on those matters that Scripture as a whole made central. While Luther taught that we cannot understand Scripture properly until the Holy Spirit opens our eyes so that we can understand it, he was also convinced that the Holy Spirit would never say anything contrary to Scripture. And so, wherever anyone felt that the Holy Spirit had spoken a truth to them, they ought immediately turn to Scripture to test the spirit to find whether, in fact, it was the Holy Spirit that was speaking or whether it was some other spirit. For Luther, then, important as the personal experience was, it could never be the finally decisive matter, it always had to be tested by something that was outside of oneself—the Scriptures.

Many people in Luther's time were claiming to have actually heard the voice of God or of an angel speaking to them. Luther, however, almost boasted of the fact that he had heard no voices. He was content to rest his case on the publicly available message of Scripture itself. There are many reasons why Luther insisted on an objective test of all experiences, no matter how vivid the experience might have been or how sure a person was of the experience. A most important reason for this was Luther's doctrine of sin.

The radical reformers, of course, also had a doctrine of sin, even a doctrine of original sin. But they had considerable confidence in the ability of the Christian to overcome sin. As a result they tended to see sin in those who disagreed with them because such ones were not truly Christian and had not had the necessary experience. And they emphasized the power that sin had had in their own lives before their conversions. Many, but not all, of the radical reformers taught that the Christian would be made perfect after conversion. George Fox, leader of the Quakers, an English expression of the radical reformation, made the claim that after his conversion he was in the perfect state from which Adam fell. [12] Even among radicals who would have found Fox's statement going too far, there was a certainty that, in the religious experiences themselves, they were protected from sin and the devil. They had no doubt that, as converted and saved Christians, they heard God's Word speaking clearly to them.

The same attitudes are common among those emphasizing religious experience today. Whether or not they preach perfection, they usually have a sublime faith that, in their experience itself, they have a direct, clear and undiluted word from God. The charismatic may confess to still having to battle sin but is confident that in the moment of speaking in tongues, sin is overcome. This experience is purely and wholly from God. What is learned in such sacred, holy experiences must be free from all taint of sin. Luther ruefully comments that some of the radicals were quite ready to question the church or the pope or even the Bible itself but they never questioned their own inner experience.

Over against the radical's view of sin, Luther put the concept of "total depravity." This term has such a disparaging ring to it in modern English that it is important to see what was implied by it at the time of the Reformation. Luther certainly did not mean that people are totally without goodness. In fact, he remained quite optimistic about how unbelievers might conduct their lives. Luther, for example, often deplored the fact that the infidel Moslems could govern themselves better than the Christians did in Germany. The doctrine of total depravity was a response to the medieval concept of the Divine gifts to human beings.

Thomas Aquinas developed the concept of the "supernatural endowment" that had been suggested by Athanasius. This distinguishes between the "natural endowments" which human beings received at creation and retained even after the Fall, and the supernatural endowments which were lost in the Fall. The supernatural endowments included the powers that enabled human beings to know God, to live according to God's will and to retain immortal life. When these endowments were lost in the Fall, humanity's natural powers of reason, conscience etc. were weakened but not destroyed. As such, they remained the image of God within fallen human beings. Fallen human beings still have the power to practice the natural virtues of prudence, justice, courage, and self control but have lost the ability to attain a vision of God or to live the Christian virtues of faith, hope, and love. Fallen humanity can regain these lost abilities only through the sacraments of the church.

The Protestant reformers, Luther and Calvin, denied any distinction between natural and supernatural endowments. They insisted that the fall had corrupted the whole of the human person. Luther insisted that when humanity fell, it lost the image of God itself. He believed that the image of God does not consist of some static set of qualities but is a matter of being oriented toward God, and thus, when humanity fell, it lost its orientation toward God and the total pattern of human life was corrupted. For Luther, therefore, "total depravity" does not mean that human beings have nothing of good left within them; it means that every aspect of human life is tainted and corrupted by the fall. Luther used his doctrine of total depravity to challenge the scholastic theology of the Middle Ages, especially its optimism with regard to reason. Following Aquinas, scholasticism believed that natural human reason, without the aid of revelation, could demonstrate that God exists, is good, is one, and so on. Although these findings of human reason could not lead to a saving relationship with God, they did provide a rational basis for receiving revelation. Luther, anticipating modern psychology's views of rationalization, saw that in fallen humanity reason tends to find the God it wants to find. Reason is always tainted by self-interest.

When Luther faced the radical reformers, he used the same doctrine of sin to throw doubt upon their reliance on experience. If our depravity is total in the sense that all aspects of our life are perverted by sin, then our experience of God, just as our reason, is tainted by our sinful nature. If self-interest causes us to find by reason the God we want to find, equally self-interest causes us to experience the God we want to experience. No matter how clearly we feel that we have experienced the Holy Spirit, we dare not close our eyes to the fact that it may be a very unholy spirit arising from the depths of our subconscious. And so Luther was convinced that we could not rely upon our experience alone, we must check it by an external criteria—God's Word in Scripture. If our experience is not in harmony with Scripture then we must count our experience as wrong, no matter how persuasive it seems to be. When people claim to have heard the voice of God or of an angel, Luther says that we must listen to them carefully. Perhaps they have a word from God and it would be presumptuous of us to ignore it. On the other hand, we cannot be gullible and take other persons at their word. The voice that they have heard may be from Satan, not God. And so we must have some criterion to test the spirit. This means that the message which purports to be from God must be tested by the word of Scripture. If the person's voice is in harmony with biblical revelation then we may accept it as a word from God. But if it contradicts scriptural revelation then, no matter how convinced the person may be that it was God who spoke, we must reject the voice as being of the devil.

But, some of the radical reformers would protest, granted that fallen human beings are corrupted in the totality of their being, converted Christians are freed from sin. Therefore, their experience is not tainted by sin. Against this objection Luther affirmed that the Christian lives as one who is at one and the same time both justified and sinful. The Christian is justified because God's forgiving love has accepted the sinner as the sinner was but the Christian is not totally freed from the power of sin.

This did not mean that Luther was pessimistic about the development of Christian life in the believer. In fact, he went so far as to say that if a person showed no signs of sanctification, that is, the development of a more Christian life, we should doubt that such a one was justified. Luther was sure that when a person had come to know the forgiving love of God's grace, it would be natural for such a person to want to do the will of God. But Luther did not believe that perfection was a human possibility. Therefore, sin would remain a problem even for the Christian. Luther also recognized that the problem tended to become more difficult as one progressed in Christian living. It was precisely the person who had made most progress in Christian living who was most tempted to become self-assured. Such people would thank God that they were not like their neighbors, and would be tempted to take for themselves the credit for their progress rather than giving the credit to God.

For Luther, therefore, an external basis for judging the experience of the Christian was always necessary. Because sin moves us to self-interested interpretations of our experience, we cannot rest upon experience. We must test our experience by the Word that God has spoken through Christ as attested to in the Scriptures. Even the Christian believer is not freed from the temptation to interpret experience in a self-seeking way. And so the Christian, in particular, will be fervent in the desire to test all experience by the scriptural witness. In this way Luther attempted to answer those who claim to be following his example in letting experience be their guide.

IV Faith and Experience in Luther

LUTHER'S CONFRONTATION WITH THE RADICAL REFORMERS led him, as we have seen, to clarify his understanding of experience and thereby to sharpen his view of the Scriptures as the primary authority for Christian faith. It also led him, as we shall see in this chapter, to clarify his understanding of the nature of faith and of how we can be certain of having it.

We have already mentioned that the Reformation was a time when people were anxiously seeking evidence to assure themselves that they were saved. Luther, in the monastery, had enthusiastically attempted to do a host of good works so that he could be assured of salvation. But always, as we have seen, Luther faced the problem that he could not be certain either that he had done enough good works or that he had done them for the right reason. And so Luther became convinced that we can never have an assurance of salvation from looking at ourselves and our works. We must look to what God has done and is doing for us. Assurance thus comes, not from looking at our works, but from looking at God's works.

At first sight, it seemed that on this point the radical reformers were solidly behind Luther. They did not depend for their salvation on their works. They followed Luther in depending on faith alone. But this raised the question of what faith is. By and large the radicals defined faith in terms of their inner feelings of the certainty of God's presence. They were confident that God had saved them because they felt saved. When, therefore, they claimed to live by faith, they meant that they were living by their daily experience of God. As a result, the radical reformers were driven to find ways of maintaining and deepening their feelings of salvation. They continually examined themselves to be sure that they still had the faith and if their experience seemed at any time to be less vibrant than before, they sought to deepen and extend their feelings of God's presence.

Luther came to see that this concern with one's experience as the proof of salvation could easily lead to a new form of salvation by works. This came out first in Luther's debate with Carlstadt, one of the radicals who tried to take the Reformation beyond Luther. Carlstadt argued that, in the Lord's Supper, one simply received bread and wine, not the body and blood of Christ. And, quoting from Paul, Carlstadt argued that flesh is of no avail (Rom. 8:5-8). For Carlstadt, the sacrament was of value only to the person who received it with "passionate, heartfelt, earnest knowledge of the body of Christ."[1] In other words, Carlstadt argued that the value of the sacrament depended on the inner feelings or experiences of the person receiving the sacrament. The sacrament was valid and efficacious only when the person receiving it felt the passionate, heartfelt knowledge of Christ. Naturally a person coming to the sacrament with such a view would be striving to experience the proper feelings. This leads Carlstadt to put emphasis upon Jesus' words, *"Do* this in remembrance of me." A person desiring to commune properly is thus urged to exert energy to remember Christ.

Luther charges that this results in making the reception of the sacrament a work to be performed to win a reward instead of a gift that is freely received. "So you can clearly see how the devil makes a commandment out of a promise of Christ and in place of faith institutes a human work. . . ."[2] The person who strives to achieve a deeper more vivid feeling of faith is, as Luther sees it, as much engaged in finding salvation within the self as the person who performs a number of outward works to attain salvation. In short, the reliance on one's feelings to give assurance of salvation is just another way of putting the self, instead of God, at the center.

One of the finest studies of Luther's theology is that of Philip Watson, *Let God Be God.* The title of Watson's book is a brilliant summary of Luther's central theological thrust. As Watson describes it, Luther brought about a "Copernican Revolution" in theology.[3] Before Copernicus people had believed that the earth was the center of the universe. Copernicus forced people to see that the sun, not the earth, was the center. In the same way, medieval theology had put human beings at the center of religious life. By doing good works people hoped to make themselves righteous before God. Luther's revolution returned God and God's works to the center. Luther called believers to "let God be God," by recognizing that God alone is the source of salvation.

As time passed, Luther saw in the radical reformers a new way of putting humanity at the center. These radicals joined Luther in extolling faith and denying the saving value of the medieval works. But, to the radicals, faith was defined so that it once more centered attention on the self. We know we are saved when we feel saved and so we must concentrate on our feelings. Instead of striving to do more works, we now try to cultivate our feelings. As Luther saw it, this is but another way of refusing to let God be God.

Luther, therefore, denied that faith is to be identified as a feeling of certainty that one is saved. Faith, he affirmed, is always God's gift, it is not something which a person might cultivate within the self. It comes as a result of hearing the good news of the Gospel and it consists of simply depending on God's promises. True faith is founded on God alone whereas a false faith comes from looking to ourselves and what we may perceive, do, or experience. As Watson sums it up, "Those whose faith is of the latter kind, if they do not experience 'external help and comfort from God', immediately imagine that God has forsaken them." [4] Such an attitude, says Luther, cannot properly be called faith at all.

Luther's view of faith leads him to the paradoxical view that faith may be most real precisely where it seems absent.

> For it happens, indeed it is so in this matter of faith, that often he who claims to believe does not at all believe; and on the other hand, he who doesn't think he believes, but is in despair, has the greatest faith. . . . [5]

Luther justifies this position by reference to Jesus' parable of the Pharisee and the Publican (Luke 18:9-14). The Pharisee was completely certain of his faith, as the pharisees in general were. On the other hand, the publican was a "miserable wretch" who could do nothing more than plead, "God have mercy upon me a sinner." And yet Jesus tells us that it was in this one, in whom faith would appear to be absent, that it was most real.

Faith, said Luther, can appear in different forms and with different degrees of strength. One person seems to trust implicitly and is untroubled by doubts. For such a one faith seems strong and triumphant over all. In another person, however, faith appears to be weak and wavering. At one moment it may be strong and confident and then in the next moment it seems to have been lost. No doubt it is more comfortable to have the strong unwavering faith and the person blessed with it ought to thank God. But, Luther insisted, it is important to see that differences in the degrees of faith do not affect the reality of a person's salvation.

Luther makes his point in an analogy. It is like two men who have a hundred gulden. One man carries his money in a poor-looking paper bag and the other carries his in a beautiful iron chest. But the hundred gulden in the beautiful chest is not worth one penny more than the hundred gulden in the paper bag. And so, says Luther, it is with Christ. Both the person with the strong faith and the person with the wavering faith have the treasure of Christ and that is all that is necessary. It is God's loving grace, offered to us in Christ, that assures us of salvation. The barest glimmer of faith is enough to cling to this gift of God. On the other hand, the strongest faith in the world is useless if it does not rest on the gift of God's grace. As a result, just as our good works are no cause for boasting or assuming that we are better than others, so also the degree of our faith is no cause for boasting and does not make us superior to another whose faith seems less strong. [6]

As one listens to the evangelistic methods of modern exponents of religious experience, one often hears the phrase "have faith!" This implies that faith is something which a person can attain by putting forth the proper effort. When Luther met this view, he branded it as a reversion to works righteousness. Faith for Luther was always a gift. This is not to imply that God somehow funnels faith into some people and not into others. Luther's point is that faith is created in the person who hears the proclamation of the Gospel. We would not say to someone "Fall in love with John or Mary." We recognize that love is born in a person as a response to who and what the other person is. Similarly, Luther wishes to emphasize that we, so to speak, "fall into faith" even as we "fall in love." Our faith in God is not something for which we can take credit anymore than we can boast of our good sense in falling in love with a particular person. The good news that God loves us, forgives us, accepts us as we are, brings about in the hearers the response of faith—a trusting attitude toward the God so proclaimed. And wherever there is aroused the barest glimmer of such trust, it is enough, says Luther.

Luther's position on faith is brought out with particular clarity in his treatise, "Concerning Rebaptism." Many of the Anabaptist groups were insisting that infant baptism is invalid because the infant cannot have faith. The Bible tells us that we are to believe and be baptized which the Anabaptist interpreted to mean that we must have faith before we can be baptized. Thus when a person had gone through the conversion experience and had the reassuring experience of God's presence, the convert was encouraged to seek baptism. In most cases, these converts had been baptized as infants into the church. But many Anabaptists did not feel that this baptism had been valid and so they sought "believer's baptism." From their point of view, they were not being rebaptized since they did not believe that their baptism as an infant had been a true baptism. But, of course, from the point of view of the Catholics, Calvinists and Anglicans, as well as of Luther, they were being rebaptized and so Luther described it in the title of his treatise.

To challenge the Anabaptist position, Luther first raised the question of how the Anabaptists could know that the child did not have faith. No Bible verse tells us this while some verses certainly imply that there is faith in some children. It is interesting to note that, in this argument Luther does not claim to know that an infant can have faith. He simply challenges his opponents to prove their claim that the infant cannot have faith.

Luther's argument that it may be possible for an infant to have faith has come in for a great deal of criticism, even in Lutheran circles. To many people it seems self-evident that an infant is incapable of having faith and so they argue that Luther must have been unsure of his case for infant baptism if he had to cling to a straw like this. But I would like to put in a dissenting voice because I think that Luther had a good point.

One reason that we have difficulty with Luther's position is because Protestants, ever since the days of Protestant orthodoxy, have tended to intellectualize faith unduly. The Reformers insisted that we are saved by God's grace, through faith. Protestant orthodoxy, which developed in the century following the Reformation, subtly changed this to salvation by grace through belief. That is, faith came to be defined in terms of believing the correct or saving doctrines. Actually this was a reversion to the medieval view which defined faith as *credentia*, the believing of what the church taught. The Reformers objected that faith is not primarily a matter of believing something but is a matter of trust, *fiducia*. To make faith a matter of believing something is to reintroduce a works righteousness. We save ourselves by putting our minds to it and believing the correct and proper things. Sometimes we even come to the conclusion that the more unbelievable a particular doctrine is, the more merit there is in our believing it. Trust on the other hand, is not something that we can generate within ourselves at will. Trust is always aroused within us as a response to another person. Because of our relationship to another person, we are moved to trust that person. Similarly, when faith in God is viewed as trusting God, it can arise within us only as a response to the nature of God in relationship to us. Here again we see why Luther spoke of faith as a gift. It cannot arise from any effort on our part but rather, as a trust in God, it is awakened or created by God's action and attitude towards us.

If faith is defined as believing certain doctrines, then Luther certainly was foolish to argue that infants may have faith. The infant, carried in a parent's arms to the baptismal font, cannot understand, let alone believe, the Apostles' Creed or Augsburg Confession. However, an infant is capable of a great deal of trust. The infant trusts the parental figures that surround it with love and care. When Luther argues that since Christ is present in baptism, his word may call forth the spirit of faith in the child, he is not thinking of an intellectual belief but of childlike trust.

Luther points out that Jesus said of children, "to such belongs the Kingdom of heaven" (Matt. 19:14). And so Jesus called his followers to become like little children. Luther argues that if these children were not, in fact, holy,

> He would indeed have given us a poor ideal with which to compare ourselves. He would not have said, you must be like children, but rather you must be otherwise than children. [7]

Since Jesus' words and actions recognize the holiness of the child and since holiness comes through faith alone, these passages clearly imply to Luther that the children in question had faith.

Luther concludes that his opponents have not been successful in establishing their premise that infants cannot have faith and hence should not be baptized. But he now turns to another argument. Even if we should grant that we cannot know whether any particular infant has faith, this does not vindicate believers' baptism. The Anabaptists emphasized the verse, "He who believes and is baptized will be saved" (Mark 16:16). They used this verse to make their case that no one should be baptized unless they first believe. But, says Luther, if you take this position, how can you ever baptize anyone? The verse does not say, "He who says that he believes and is baptized shall be saved, but he who believes." [8] How can anyone know that the person who claims to have faith really does have faith? Luther asks, "Have they now become gods so that they can discern the hearts of men and know whether or not they believe?" [9] Here Luther charges that there is a basic contradiction in the position of the Anabaptists. On the one hand they refuse to accept the validity of infant baptism because they cannot know that the child has faith, then they turn around and blithely baptize adults even though they still have no way of knowing that such ones have the faith that they claim to have. "To have his confession is not to know his faith. With all your reasoning you cannot do justice to this verse unless you know that he has faith since all men are liars and God alone knows the heart." [10] Again, Luther reminds his readers that Jesus said that not everyone who says "Lord, Lord" will enter the kingdom (Matt. 7:21). But, in practicing believers' baptism, Luther argues, the Anabaptists are taking the word of anyone who says "Lord, Lord."

Luther recognizes that the persons presenting themselves for baptism are convinced that they do have faith. They experience the inner assurance of a faith relationship with God. But the problem, as Luther well knew from his own experience, is that such feelings of assurance have a way of coming and going. One day faith seems strong and real but often the next day it seems weak, wavering and even nonexistent. Does this mean that the faith has been lost? Or does it indicate that it never had been true faith? If so, and on the third day faith again seems real should the person be rebaptized? Once you have opened the way to rebaptizing people, where do you stop? How many times may it be necessary to rebaptize someone before you can be sure that they really did have faith and that hence the baptism was valid?

From these considerations Luther concludes that these questions and absurdities arise whenever we base the validity of baptism on the faith and experience of the person being baptized. He concludes, therefore, that "Faith does not exist for the sake of baptism but baptism for the sake of faith. When faith comes, baptism is complete." [11]

It is a well-known fact that when Luther was in doubt and despair he would say to himself, "I have been baptized." This was not a superstitious belief in the magical power of the baptismal act. What Luther was saying was that his relationship to God did not depend on how he felt about God. Somedays God seemed very real and loving to Luther and on other days God seemed very remote, unloving, and judgmental. [12] Luther came to know that he could not live by such changing feelings within himself. He discovered that the important thing was not how Luther felt or how strong Luther's faith was but how God felt about Luther. And God's attitude to Luther had been expressed in baptism whereby God made the covenant with Luther. In baptism, God's grace had reached forth and embraced Luther, sealing the covenant with the promise of God's unchanging steadfast, forgiving love. Baptism, therefore, was to Luther the concrete symbol of God's acceptance of the unacceptable. By reminding himself that he had been baptized, Luther was able, in Tillich's words "to accept his acceptance." This was possible because baptism reminded him that his relationship to God did not depend on his weak, sinful vacillating feelings, it depended on what God had done for him. Only in this way can we let God be God. To seek baptism on the basis of our faith would be a new way of putting the self and not God at the center.

From this discussion of Luther's development of faith in the context of the discussion on baptism, it is evident why Luther saw in an experience-centered religion the danger of a return to works righteousness. The essence of works righteousness is that we believe it is up to us to achieve our position and status with God. People who believe that they have performed the necessary requirements are then tempted to thank God that they are not like those who have not achieved the same goals. The Reformers were all agreed that the kind of works called good by the Roman Catholic Church of the time were not a way to salvation. Indulgences, pilgrimages, giving money to build churches and all of the rest were not ways to earn the favor and good will of God. But some of the Protestants, Luther feared, were using their particular experiences to assure themselves that they had met the requirement of salvation and were hence thanking God that they were not like those who had not achieved them.

As Luther saw it, the Anabaptists believed that they could be baptized only when their faith was strong, and so they tried to cultivate their faith in order that they could be worthy of baptism. Luther insisted that we should be baptized precisely because our faith is weak or nonexistent and to Luther that was the whole distinction between works righteousness and justification by grace through faith. Luther sums it up,

> There is, however, a devil who promotes confidence in works among them. He feigns faith, whereas he really has a work in mind. He uses the name and guise of faith to lead the poor people to rely on a work. Just as it happened under the papacy when we were driven to the sacrament as a work of obedience . . . , so here again the Anabaptists are urging on to a work so that when the people are baptized they may have confidence that everything is right and complete. [13]

This comparison of the reliance on experience to works righteousness is helpful in bringing out more fully Luther's attitude to experience. When Luther attacked work righteousness, his Roman Catholic critics charged that Luther was opposed to good works. This, of course, was to make Luther sound dangerously indifferent to ethical concerns. Luther, throughout his life, was at great pains to emphasize that in no way was he opposed to good works. It greatly disturbed him to see people using his teachings (as they had used Paul's) to justify themselves in sinning so that grace might abound. Luther was certain that where there is Christian faith there will be works of Christian love and action that will follow from it. The problem was not that there is anything wrong with good works, although Luther was not sure that many of the works extolled by the medieval church were truly good. The basic problem was that people were made to feel that their acceptance by God was contingent on their performing the good works. Luther's whole point was that the good works are the fruits of our relationship to God and not the roots of that relationship. Instead of saying that we are saved because we have performed good works, we come to see that we are only able to perform good works because we are saved.

Luther sees a similar theme in the question of religious experience. In no way does Luther wish to disparage the glory and the wonder of experiencing God, God's presence, God's grace and God's love. Luther was certain that the work of God in Christ was unavailing to anyone until it was possible to see that what had been done was done *"for me."* This personal appropriation of Christ's work certainly implies an experiential relationship to God in Christ. But, just as Luther believed that good works would follow from the justifying relationship with God and should not be depended on as the basis for justification, similarly, Luther believed that one's experience of God's grace followed from justification and was not the cause or basis for it.

This comes out even more clearly as we examine Luther's experience of God. His first such experience is described by scholars in the German word, *anfechtung.* This was the experience of the holiness, the otherness, the righteousness of God. For Luther this was a terrifying experience because as he experienced God's holy righteousness, he was at the same time struck with an overwhelming sense of his own unworthiness. He became aware that he stood under the judgment of the righteous God. In this experience he faced the hopelessness of the task of fulfilling the demands of God. To experience *anfechtung* was to experience despair inasmuch as one experienced being under judgment with no power to remove it.

It was not, for Luther, a simple case in which the experience of *anfechtung* came to him only before his discovery of the biblical message of justification. On the contrary, he continued throughout his life to experience it. As Karl Holl describes it, ". . . these *Anfechtungen* always took Luther by surprise. This confirms his view that genuine religion originates in an experience of the divine that is neither sought nor desired. Suddenly, unexpectedly, in the stillness of the night the Numinous is there!" [14] Whenever Luther experienced *anfechtung* he needed to retrace his original steps of looking again to the promises made in Christ of God's willingness to forgive, he needed to remind himself that he had been baptized. Because Luther's experience of *anfechtung* was so persistent, he could never rely on his own religious feelings for assurance, he needed to find the external objective assurance of God's promises in the Scripture. And so Luther came to distinguish faith from experience. He could say, "God is not to be known through feeling but faith." [15] That is, faith was not seen by Luther as the experience of God's presence but the relationship that is born from out of trusting the promises of God.

Luther was sure that, where there is faith, Christ is always present in the believer. He says, "When we believe that Christ came *for us*, he dwells in our hearts by such faith and purifies us daily by his own proper work." [16] And, to have Christ indwelling is to have the presence of the Holy Spirit as a power within our lives to make us holy. Luther says, in his *Large Catechism* that to say in the Creed that one believes in the Holy Spirit means "I believe that the Holy Spirit makes me holy, as his name implies." [17] Here too, however, Luther makes it clear that the Holy Spirit's work is not a matter of feeling. The means through which the Holy Spirit makes us holy are "the Christian church, the forgiveness of sins, the resurrection of the body, and the life everlasting."

We can sum up this chapter by saying that for Luther the experience of God was real and important. It was real in the sense of *anfechtung* whereby one knows one's unworthiness and perilous state before the judgment of God. It was real in the experience of the indwelling Christ as the Holy Spirit that brings a sense of peace from having been accepted by God. But true and abiding assurance can no more come from looking at our personal experience than it can come from looking at the good works we may perform. Assurance comes only when we look outside of ourselves to the objective work that God has done and is doing. Faith, therefore, is never a *feeling* of assurance, for such feelings come and go. Faith is the trust that is given by the Holy Spirit whereby we have confidence that God will keep the promises made in Christ.

The church has often been disturbed and divided by the issue of experience. Persons who have had particular experiences of God (the "born again experience", speaking in tongues, etc.) often claim that they alone are Christian. They refuse to recognize others as Christians until they have had (or claim to have had) the same experience. On the other hand, those whose experience of God has been different often look upon those with these particular experiences as dangerous oddities. The first group tends often to leave congregations that include people who have not had its particular experience and to form or join congregations where everyone shares the same experience. The second group often tends to freeze out or force out the first group as a demonic influence.

Luther offers a way around these controversies. The important and crucial element of Christianity is faith. Faith is created by God's action in Christ and consists of trusting God to keep the promises made through Christ. Where there is faith there will be experiences of God but these are gifts given by God and are not a sign of higher or better faith. If God has not chosen to give the same experiences to all of the faithful, that is no reason for the faithful to exclude each other. Once we understand that our justification is linked to faith, not to experience, we can thank God for the experience we have received without thanking God that we are not like our neighbor who did not receive the same experience.

Luther's Theology V of the Cross and Experience

CENTRAL TO LUTHER'S UNDERSTANDING OF THE GOSPEL was what he called the "theology of the cross." For Luther this was not a particular doctrine but a perspective or motif that enables us to understand all Christian doctrines. The essence of the theology of the cross is that God always comes to us in ways that we do not expect and which, at first sight, seem disappointing or inappropriate. This theme was expressed by Paul when he said, "For Jews demand signs and Greeks seek wisdom, but we preach Christ crucified, a stumbling block to Jews and folly to Gentiles, but to those who are called, both Jews and Greeks, Christ the power of God and the wisdom of God (1 Cor. 1:22-24).

Luther developed his theology of the cross by contrasting it to the "theology of glory" which he found to be dominant in the church of his time. This terminology is often confusing today because "glory" is a good word in Christian circles. We speak of the glory of God, the glory of the Christian life and so on. Because glory is a good word, the contrast of a theology of the cross and a theology of glory easily leads to the assumption that we need a proper balance between the two. But to Luther this would have been as perverse as attempting to get a balance between salvation by works and salvation by grace alone. And it would have been perverse for the same reasons inasmuch as Luther's theology of the cross is implied by his understanding of justification, and he believed that a theology of glory always underlies belief in works righteousness. Perhaps Luther too found that the term "theology of glory" was misleading since he used it less in his later writings. We can bring out Luther's meaning better if we substitute the term "triumphalism" for "theology of glory."

The essence of triumphalism is to believe that God is most clearly evident in the successes, certainties and victories of life. Triumphalism is always confident of its ability to know and serve God and is certain that God will reward such service. Luther found triumphalism penetrating the church of his day. It was a time when miracle stories abounded and miracles were seen as proving the truth of the church's teachings and demonstrating the merit of those who profited by the miracles. The works righteousness that Luther attacked was based upon the triumphalist assumption that human beings have sufficient goodness within themselves to earn merit with God. Following Thomas Aquinas, the church had a triumphalist confidence in the ability of human reason to demonstrate the existence of God and to learn much about God's nature. Also it was believed that human reason was capable of discovering the moral code God had willed for all humanity. This church had such a triumphalist confidence in its possession of the truth of God's revelation that it felt justified in conducting the Inquisition and other forms of oppression to protect this truth from what it deemed to be heresy. In extolling the monastic way of life, the church expressed its belief that, with God's help, certain saints were capable of living a life so righteous that they could earn a surplus of merit that could be distributed to the less righteous.

Triumphalism appears to be natural to human beings. One of the roots of all religion is the desire to win supernatural help in achieving goals. The history of religions abounds with gods and goddesses who give aid in hunting, victory in war, fertility, healing, prosperity, and the like. People have readily changed the deities they worship when other deities seemed better able to deliver the desired benefits. When in ancient times a nation was defeated in war, it was assumed that the only sensible thing to do was to worship the gods and goddesses of the victors since these were proven by the victory to be more powerful and effective.

The history of the Jews stands out in opposition at this point. For example, when the Jews were carried into captivity in Babylon, it would be expected that they would quit worshiping Yahweh and worship instead Marduk, Ishtar, and other Babylonian deities. That they did not do so was a mark of the uniqueness of the Jewish faith. The Jews did not see their defeat as a proof of the superiority of the Babylonion gods. They saw it as a means whereby Yahweh was punishing them for their sins and so they retained the faith that Yahweh would deliver them from captivity in Yahweh's own good time. In other words, the Jews' faith in Yahweh never depended upon triumphs. Yahweh, they believed, was present in adversity as well as in victory.

As Luther sees it, biblical revelation disappoints all of the triumphal human expectations of religion. In the Bible, God is always manifest in unexpected ways and so it is, paradoxically, that even in revelation God is hidden as well as revealed. God does not appear in glory and majesty but in a humble, hidden way in the person of Jesus. Luther says that Philip spoke according to a theology of glory when he asked Jesus to show them the Father (John 14:8). "Christ forthwith set aside his flighty thought about seeing God elsewhere and led him to himself saying, 'Philip, he who has seen me has seen the Father'."[1] Where the human expectation is that God will appear with supernatural and miraculous evidence, in Jesus God comes as a child born in a lowly manger and nursed at Mary's breast. God does not appear as a king, a person of authority, or a brilliant scholar. God comes as a lowly carpenter who sees the idea of ruling over others as a temptation of the devil (Luke 4:5-8). Jesus did not have a life of success and victory; on the contrary, he had no place to lay his head although foxes have holes and birds have nests (Matt. 8:20). Jesus had a brief period of popularity, but he was soon deserted by the crowds and at the end even his disciples deserted him. He died the most despicable and humiliating death that the Romans could invent.

It might be objected that Jesus was resurrected and that, in light of this triumphalist ending, the seriousness of the cross is overcome. But it is vital to see that the resurrection was not a triumph as the world counts triumph. Jesus did not appear victoriously to Pilate or Caiaphas to confront them with their sins or to win them to discipleship. The risen Christ did not appear to the crowds to demonstrate publicly that Jesus always had been right and his crucifiers wrong. The resurrected Christ only appeared to a few disciples and friends in relatively obscure and nonpublic places. Early in his career Jesus rejected as a temptation of Satan the use of miracles to win popular following (Matt. 4:5-7). At the end of his earthly career Jesus did not succumb to the same temptation. If a triumph was wanted, Hollywood could have written a much better script.

Popular presentation of the life of Jesus today usually emphasize his miracles in a way that results in a triumphal proof of Jesus' divinity. But Luther took a different view. Luther considered that Jesus' miracles were the least important of his works, "For the devil was defeated by weakness, not magnificent miracles." [2] Luther lived in a time when reports of recent miracles abounded on all sides, yet he was unpersuaded that such miracles could validate the theological beliefs of the miracle workers. Luther also noted that miracles did not win followers in Jesus' own lifetime. [3] In fact, to some they were witnesses of Jesus' satanic nature (Matt. 12:24). Luther believed that Jesus' obvious reluctance to perform miracles except where human need desperately required them arose because the popular attention to miracles interfered with his main work—teaching.

For Luther the greatest of miracles, in light of which all other miracles receded into the background, was that God came to us in one who was fully and completely a human being. Luther never tired of emphasizing the human frailty of Jesus. His references to Christmas abound in descriptions of the weakness and helplessness of the baby Jesus. Jesus grew in stature and knowledge like any other child (Luke 2:52). Through Christian history a number of legends have developed to demonstrate that even in childhood Jesus had omnipotent powers and omniscient knowledge. Luther branded such accounts as "inane and blasphemous drivel." [4] As an adult, Jesus lived a fully human life. Unlike the monastics, Jesus was not poor because of a vow to poverty but from the necessities of his situation. He grew tired, hungry, and eventually he died. He lived a life of serving others rather than of being served.

Although Luther goes out of his way to describe the full and complete humanity of Jesus, this in no way detracted from Luther's conviction that God was fully present in the life, death, and resurrection of Jesus. Luther stood firmly on the principle that the finite is capable of receiving the infinite and hence it is precisely in the finite human person that the infinite

God dwelt. And so Luther can affirm, "Yet these two natures are so united that there is only one God and Lord, that Mary suckles God with her breasts, bathes God, rocks him, and carries him; furthermore, that Pilate and Herod crucified and killed God. The two natures are so joined that the true deity and humanity are one." [5]

It is evident that for Luther the theology of the cross is not simply a way of looking at Jesus' death. The actual crucifixion of Jesus is the culmination of what is involved in the whole of his life. The cross illustrates the way of God with humanity. A major reason why Jesus was rejected was because he did not come to the world in a triumphal way. "They would not listen to Him, because they were steeped in the illusion that the Messiah would come attended by a host of warriors. If Christ had entered Jerusalem in great splendor and had announced that he was the Christ, they would have fallen down before him and accepted him." [6]

Because Jesus is the revelation of God, the theology of the cross describes the nature of God. By coming to the world in the human suffering form of Jesus, God is revealed as one who loves and suffers with humanity. Throughout the history of Christianity there has been a strong tradition, influenced by Greek philosophy, which has insisted that God cannot suffer. Because God is omnipotent and perfect, God cannot lack any desired thing and hence cannot suffer. From this it is concluded that Jesus suffered in his humanity but not in his divinity. Luther is harsh in his judgment of this view. "Many heretics have arisen . . . who have assailed this article of faith and have been offended at the thought that God should suffer. The Godhead, they argued, is an eternal majesty . . . God cannot be crucified! But tell him that this person, who is God and man, was crucified." [7]

Because a theology of the cross describes God and the revelation through Christ, the church and the Christian life are to be patterned after the cross. Along with many in his day, Luther deplored the political power and wealth which the church of the time possessed. Luther contrasted this to the early church as he recalled how Jesus gathered the first disciples.

> He refrained from calling the high priests and rulers into his ranks. He gave the nation's sovereign the cold shoulder, and he did not invite men of distinction. He journeyed through the wilderness, through hamlets and market towns, and selected the poorest and the most wretched beggars He could find, such as poor fishermen and good, simple uncouth bumpkins. It almost seems as though He felt unable to administer His kingdom unless He surrounded Himself with such simple folk." [8]

The church so gathered was not showered with wealth, comfort, and ease. On the contrary, following Christ meant taking up the cross and so most of the disciples, like their Lord, were put to death. The church was called to serve, not to be exalted. Suffering for the sake of Christ rather than possessing pomp and riches is the mark of the true church.

Applied to the church, the theology of the cross means that even as God was hidden in the human form of Jesus, so the true church is always hidden in unimpressive expressions. The world expects that, if Christianity is true, the church will be marked by triumphal proofs of its faith and purity. It expects to see evidence of worldly success and it expects to see heroic examples of piety. The church in Luther's time presented the first in its pomp, wealth, and political power and the second in its monastic orders. Over against this, Luther affirmed that the works of the true church "are no more than what even non-Christians and knaves are able to do." [9] The non-Christians often have better forms of government than Christian lands, heretics have frequently lived stricter lives than the orthodox. [10] The true church is not to be located by looking at any observable and triumphant kind of works. The true church exists where there is faith and dependence on Christ alone.

Similarly, the true church is not to spend its efforts in works of an impressively religious nature. As is natural to human nature, the church of Luther's time believed that it had to express its Christian faith by doing something that was "different and out of the ordinary." And so the church had cultivated extraordinary pursuits like entering a cloister, denying the needs of the body, practicing celibacy etc. Over against this, Luther insists that the truly Christian life is a life lived in the world through faith in Christ. "And all their life and everything they do is called good fruit, even if it were something more menial than when a farm hand loads and hauls manure." [11] Thus Christians are not called to extraordinary and seemingly "spiritual" works. They are called to the common tasks of being good fathers, mothers, farmers, storekeepers and any other vocation necessary to the welfare of society.

In her or his own life the Christian is not to seek or expect special benefits or privileges. Luther would have been strongly opposed to those modern forms of Christianity whose evangelism so often consists primarily of making extravagant promises of the rewards to be gained when one "accepts Christ." Luther believed that, as God came humbly in the unexpectably human Jesus, so the life of a Christian often appears to be denial of the presence of God. Suffering is more often the mark of the Christian than rewards. It is part of our human sin that we assume we know what is good for us and hence when our prayers are answered, we assume that it is a sign of God's favor toward us. But Luther disagrees. In Romans 8:26 Paul says, "For we do not know how to pray." From this Luther concludes that "It is not a bad sign, but a very good one, if things turn out contrary to our requests. Just as it is not a good sign if everything turns out favorably for our requests." [12] Even as God is hidden in the humanity of Jesus, so God is hidden in the seemingly unanswered prayer.

We have made this rather extensive summary of Luther's theology of the cross because it underlies much of what he has to say about experience. Paul Althaus summarizes the differences between a theology of glory and a theology of the cross in the following terms: "The theology of glory seeks to know God directly in his obviously divine power, wisdom, and glory; whereas the theology of the cross paradoxically recognizes him precisely where he has hidden himself, in his sufferings and in all that which the theology of glory considers to be weakness and foolishness." [13] This quotation provides a useful key to the understanding of Luther's view on experience.

Experience is seen as providing a direct and unmediated knowledge of God and relationship to God. Many of those whom Luther critcized in his day believed that the Holy Spirit had spoken directly to them in their experience and had given them direct instructions for action and assurance of their own salvation. Luther could say that a person who had such a viewpoint "has devoured the Holy Spirit feathers and all." [14] Luther, as we have emphasized before, was not opposed to the religious experiences of Christians. He was opposed to this triumphalist confidence in experience as an unmediated way to the "divine power, wisdom, and glory."

Luther believed that the God who comes to us by way of the cross deals with us in a twofold manner: first outwardly and then inwardly. First God approaches us by the word of preaching and teaching the sacraments and the written Scriptures. Only after this do we receive the inner experience of the Holy Spirit. "God has determined to give the inward to no one except through the outward." [15] Triumphalism, however, always wants to reverse the order and to make the inner experience primary so that often the outward is seen as inferior and unnecessary. Mere water, as in baptism, cannot cleanse us, only the Spirit can do that. So the basic question is not whether you have been baptized with the Word and water, but whether you have been baptized by the Holy Spirit. Bread and wine are of no profit; we must meet God spiritually. The inner life must therefore be developed, we must listen for the heavenly voice to speak within us; we must cultivate the inner spirituality. Thus Luther can sum it up by saying that the triumphalist "wants to teach you, not how the Spirit comes to you but how you come to the Spirit." [16]

Luther developed this theme constantly throughout his writing and he brings it together in an interesting way in his exegesis of John, chapters 14-16 where Jesus speaks at length about the Holy Spirit. We shall follow Luther's development of his thought in this context.

Luther's discussion of the Holy Spirit presupposes the Trinity. The oneness of God is affirmed even as the three persons of the Trinity are emphasized. Because God is one, God's action in Christ and God's action through the Spirit are completely integrated and in harmony. Triumphalism always looks for obvious and glorious marks of the presence of the Holy Spirit. It expects evidence of worldly success and inward illumination. But, just as a theology of the cross is based upon the fact that God was hidden in the humble human person of Jesus, so too, the Holy Spirit is hidden within the frailty of human flesh. Several times in these three chapters of John Jesus emphasizes that his disciples are soon to face suffering, persecution, sorrow, and trials (e.g. see John 15:18-21; 16:2, 20). Luther picks up these references and emphasizes that the Christian's life always involves sufferings. Not only is the Christian subject to all the woes and misfortunes which are the common lot of humanity but the Christian suffers even more. "He feels nothing but sheer terror and sadness within; and without he feels hatred, envy, shame, and persecution by the world, yes even by his own closest friends." When the Christian asks why there is not a single hour of peace on the earth, the answer comes, "If I had not been baptized and had not accepted the Gospel, I would not be so wretched." [17]

In the midst of these sufferings, feelings or inner experience are not a reliable support or guide. Triumphalism promises that no matter what happens to us, if we have faith God's presence will always be experienced as a reality that upholds and strengthens us. But Luther found that it was not so and Jesus had not promised that it would be so. "Anyone who is deeply rooted and well-grounded will often imagine that he has neither God nor Christ. He will feel nothing but death, the devil, and sin passing over him like a violent storm and a dark cloud." [18] But these feelings are unreliable because "at such times he will not be forsaken, as it seems." In other words, as God comes to us in the unexpectably human form of Jesus, so God comes as Holy Spirit in the unexpected situation in which our feelings tell us that we are abandoned.

The presence of the Holy Spirit, the Comforter, with us is not verified by some intense or ecstatic feeling or inner experience. The presence of the Holy Spirit is attested by the fact that, despite the external evils and the inner disturbance, we retain our faith in Christ. For, as Luther sees it, the Holy Spirit has one basic office, to kindle and preserve faith in Christ. The Holy Spirit is not a separate divinity, coming with some new or different revelation. The God who came to us in Christ is the same God who comes as the Holy Spirit.

Through Christian history, it has not been unusual to find Christians who are firmly rooted in a theology of the cross insofar as they interpret Christ. They affirm that God came hidden in the human form of Christ who died on the cross. But when they turn to the Holy Spirit, they become triumphalist. They believe that in the Holy Spirit they see God face to face, no longer veiled and hidden in the human form. Luther's understanding of the Trinity and his exegesis of Jesus' teachings would not let him follow this path. The theology of the cross applies just as completely to God the Holy Spirit as it does to God the Son. The Holy Spirit does not illuminate us with an unearthly glory, it establishes faith in Christ. In the last chapter we saw that Luther taught that faith is a gift. Here we can see that it is the Holy Spirit that makes the gift. But the faith is always faith in Christ. The Holy Spirit is manifested through the faith in Christ which sustains the Christian.

How does the Holy Spirit come to us? Luther emphasizes that it comes through the preaching of the Word, the study of Scripture, and the sacraments. Christians are like the Children of Israel when they crossed the Red Sea. The Israelites, on approaching the water could see no means of getting over. They had to rely on the promise that God had made to them. In the same way for the Christian, "there is nothing visible or evident to indicate that this is the way that leads to eternal life, since man feels only terror and the fear of death. But, over against this, Christ stands with his words as he says: 'I am the Way.' " [19] Just as God was present in the human Jesus, God is present today in the human words of preaching that tell again the good news that came with Christ and in the sacraments administered by the human church.

Triumphalism always wants something more than these human words on which it can rely. It wants a direct vision and experience of God in divine glory that will banish all doubts and fears. But, says Luther, on this earth, it is not to be.

> When we get to heaven, we shall see God differently; then no clouds and no darkness will obscure our view. But here on earth we shall not perceive Him with our senses and our thoughts. No, here we see Him, as St. Paul states (1 Cor. 13:12), "in a mirror dimly," enveloped in an image, namely in the Word and the sacraments. These are His masks or His

garments, as it were, in which He conceals Himself. But He is certainly present in these, Himself working miracles, preaching, administering the sacraments, consoling, strengthening and helping. We see Him as we see the sun through a cloud. [20]

This passage is an eloquent expression of the theology of the cross as it applies to Christian knowledge and experience of God in this life. The proclamation of the Word and the sacraments are based on the Incarnation itself. God comes to us through these earthly forms of expression as God came to us in the human person of Jesus.

Another aspect of Luther's theology of the cross is that the Word of God, coming to us from out of the incarnation of Christ and mediated by proclamation and sacraments, is only really comprehended as we face adversity. "Even though we hear it, it fails to take root until trials bring it home to us; we must learn it when death wrestles with us or when any other affliction oppresses and frightens us." [21] Triumphalism looks for assurance in being delivered from the afflictions of life. But a theology of the cross finds that the Holy Spirit's presence is made real in the midst of suffering. In the fires of trial, the Word comes to us and we find that we do believe and trust and are able to bear the afflictions.

Here it is obvious that Luther is speaking of experience but in a different sense than is so often meant when we speak of religious experience. In an earlier chapter I spoke of the view that religious experience is any experience of a person who is religious. It would seem that Luther would agree with that. One comes to see the daily events of life, particularly those that bring fears and afflictions, in light of the gospel. Understanding is awakened in the mind and heart. The vital experience for the Christian is not some ecstatic inner feeling of God's presence, rather it is the ordinary everyday experience through which we come to see

God's presence. As the Word appeared in the human life of Jesus in a purely human setting, so the Holy Spirit is manifested in and through the purely human experience.

At this point it is necessary again to remind ourselves that Luther in no way denied the reality of the inner sense of communion with God that the Christian experiences. Luther himself knew this experience and has many beautiful things to say about it. For example, near the end of this treatment of John 14-16, Luther says, "Accordingly, having peace in him means nothing else than this: he who has Christ's Word in his heart becomes so bold and unafraid that he can scorn and defy the devil's wrath and raging." [22] Luther's concern is not to discourage inner experience but to set it in the proper perspective. As seen in the earlier quotation, Luther insisted that the first work of the Holy Spirit is the outward one of proclaiming the Word and administering the sacraments and that the inner work of the Holy Spirit is secondary and only comes after the first.

There are two reasons for Luther's insistence on this order in the work of the Holy Spirit. First of all, he wants it clearly understood that we cannot depend on our inner experience alone. Inner experiences come and go and differ in strength and intensity. Often as the Christian looks to her or his experience, the absence and unreality of God is all that is experienced. Worse yet, as Luther knew full well from his own experience, often the only thing that our inner feelings attest is the wrath of God in light of our many shortcomings and sins. It is necessary that in such moments the Christian be able to turn to a firm assurance that comes from outside the self. This is found in the life and teaching of Jesus as proclaimed in the words of the church and the sacraments. When one holds firmly to these outward promises, only then may the inner assurance come.

This order of the outward first and the inward second is put clearly in the following passage which is in answer to the question of how Christians can stand in face of the trials, tribulations, and doubts that they face.

> From what source will Christians draw the strength and the courage to overcome this? Solely from Christ's assurance: "I am in you and you in me, and we are united in everything. Therefore hold firmly to me! Through My Word I have made the beginning and have brought you to me. And now if you prove this, if you fight to remain in Me, you will be greatly troubled at first, and it will be difficult for you. It will seem that you are alone and that I have forsaken you and am abandoning you to fear and all wretchedness. But just hold fast, and I will prove that I love you. Then you will feel in your hearts how pleasing your faith, your confession, and your suffering are to God. And from this you will recognize and experience even better who I am, how powerful I am, and what I am working in you." [23]

Luther's second reason for this order is even more important. If we let our inner experience become primary, we shall soon begin to trust in ourselves and to turn away from faith in Christ. We easily slip into confidence in our experience so that Christ, the preaching of his Word and the sacraments all fade to the periphery and seem less than essential. Luther saw this happening in many of the groups in his time, even as we can see it today. When this happens we have returned to a works righteousness. Again and again Luther insists that we cannot look to ourselves to find assurance of place before God. Against the Roman Catholic Church of his day he emphasized that we cannot find assurance by looking at the works we perform, and against the radical wing of the Reformation he insisted that we cannot gain assurance from looking at our experience of God. Only when we look outside of ourselves to what God has done for us in Christ can we find assurance.

When the Christian looks to Christ alone and receives the

100 Luther's Theology of the Cross and Experience

gift of faith, Luther was certain that good works would follow. It is as natural for faith to produce works of love and service as it is for a vine to bear fruit. Likewise Luther was convinced that where there is faith, there would follow the inner experience of God's presence in God's own good time. But in both cases, the order was crucial. If works or experience were put before faith, we were again in the situation where our salvation is found within ourselves rather than in God's attitude toward us. And so he sums it up, "The Holy Spirit wants this truth (the teaching of Scripture) which he is to impress into our hearts to be so firmly fixed that reason and all one's own thoughts and feelings are relegated to the background." [24]

There is another aspect in which the theology of the cross influences Luther's view of the place of experience. The theology of the cross puts a high evaluation on the material world. Centered in the Word that became flesh, emphasizing the humanity of Jesus, depending on the spoken word and the water, bread and wine of the sacraments, the theology of the cross sees the material world as having a central place in God's plan. Triumphalism does not necessarily disparage the material world. In fact, some forms of triumphalism identify material wealth with God's gifts and see it as a proof of the owner's righteousness. However, many of the forms of triumphalism that Luther faced did disparage the material world over against "spiritual" things. Such a view is usually associated with an emphasis on inner religious experience. Inasmuch as the inner experiences seem independent of material things, it is deemed to be more spiritual. Thus the inner experience is held to be more pleasing to God and more God-filled than words of proclamation or the material elements used in the sacraments.

This disparagement of the material world and the exaltation of the "spiritual" is so widespread in human history that we have to conclude that it appeals to something deep in the human psyche. It is found in Hindu and Buddhist forms of religion. It has had a persisting influence over Christianity because it was prominent in some of the Greek schools of philosophy that have influenced Christians through the centuries.

The disparagement of the material is based on a dualistic view of reality. There is the material world on the one hand and on the other there is the spiritual world. The material world is evil or, at least, a very poor vehicle for the concerns of the spiritual world. The spiritual world is good and always intimately related to the divine.

Luther's theology of the cross led him to interpret the Scripture in a way that modern biblical studies have verified. The Bible does not have a dualistic view of either matter and spirit or body and soul. Luther recognized that the Bible presents the human person as a whole or a unity, not a duality. In a passage in which he is explaining the Incarnation, Luther illustrates the unity of Christ by using the unity of the human being as an analogy. He says,

> You cannot indicate a special place or space where the soul is present alone without the body, like a kernel without the shell, or where the flesh is without the skin, like a pea without a pod. On the contrary, wherever the one is, there must the other be also. Thus you cannot shell the divinity from the humanity and lay it aside at some place away from the humanity. [25]

Over against this view, of course, several passages from Paul can be quoted where he speaks of the flesh as evil and the spirit as good. At first sight, these passages sound as though Paul is teaching the traditional Greek dualism of body and soul. However, again like modern biblical scholars, Luther recognizes that in such passages Paul is using the term "flesh" not to describe the material body but to refer to a human being living apart from Christ. Thus, discussing 1 Cor. 15:50 where Paul says that "Flesh and blood cannot inherit the kingdom" Luther comments, "Here 'flesh' means a carnal mind, will, understanding or self-contrived opinion, as Paul in Rom. 8:6 says, 'To set the mind on the flesh is death.'" [26] Luther's view is confirmed when we look at the list of the works of the flesh as Paul describes them in Gal. 5:19-21. Here we find that Paul includes some things which, from a dualistic point of view, would be fruits of the physical body— licentiousness, drunkenness and carousing. However, the majority of the fruits of the flesh deal with matters that, in a dualistic theory, would come from the spirit or soul—idolatry, sorcery, enmity, strife, jealousy, anger, selfishness, dissension, party spirit and envy. Obviously Paul is not working here with a body-soul dualism, he is thinking of the "flesh" as a description of the whole self as it lives outside of faith. Luther's term, "carnal mind," seems a good summary.

On the other hand, Luther affirmed that the works of the "Spirit" bear no relation to a body-soul dualism. Instead, ". . . all that our body does outwardly and physically, if God's Word is added to it and it is done through faith, is in reality and in name done spiritually." [27] This means first of all for Luther that the material elements of the sacraments—water, bread and wine— take on spiritual significance when the Word is added to them. Those who disdain the material elements of the sacraments in order to be more spiritual have thus missed the biblical meaning of "spiritual." Luther charges that Carlstadt, for example, "is bent on making spiritual what God wants to be bodily." [28]

The emphasis of Luther on the spiritual working through matter and the body results in more than a defense of the sacraments. He also argues that God is most truly served through the every-day material world and its operations. The triumphalist, trying to be spiritual, assumes that activities must be found which are "different and out of the ordinary" and such a one turns to the ascetic or celibate way of life which denies the physical and material expressions. "And they are quick to deduce from this that rearing children, doing domestic work, etc. is not a holy life. For they look solely at the outward appearance of the works and are unable to judge by the source of these works and their origin in the Vine." [29] What marks a work as spiritual and pleasing to God is not a question of whether it is a work of the "soul" or of the body, it is a question of the motive behind it. When it is done out of faith in God, it is a good work no matter how humble and ordinary it may seem.[30]

It needs to be remembered that Luther had two prongs in his attack on "good works" in the medieval church. On the one hand, as is well known, he insisted that no works of ours could win, earn, or deserve salvation. That depends on God alone. But, less well known, was his claim that the medieval church had the wrong concept of what good works are. It supposed that good works are those which a person does directly for God, hence they are "spiritual" in nature—fasting, saying prayers, giving to the church, going on pilgrimages, entering the monastery, etc. Against this Luther argued that God, the almighty creator, needs nothing that we could give. Truly good works, therefore, are works for those whom God loves—our neighbors. In a typical passage Luther says that we always want to reverse the proper order. Instead of accepting favors from God, we want to do favors for God and so we "erect buildings, endow and sacrifice" to win God's favor. "On the other hand, when we are asked to give to our neighbor who is in need of our help, and to do good to him, we will not and cannot do or give anything. In brief, we refuse to accept anything from God and we refuse to give others anything." [31] Lutheran ethics do not call a person out of the world to some kind of sacred or spiritual activity but rather they send one into the world to serve the neighbor through the tasks that are at hand.

Dualistic world views usually do not have a doctrine of creation such as we find in Scripture. Usually they see the spiritual world and matter both existing from eternity and the creating gods simply bring the two together. Since matter is a poor medium for the works of the spirit, the spiritual person tries to overcome and escape from the body. For Luther, the material world is God's creation, it is essentially good, it is meant for use in line with God's purposes. To call something spiritual, therefore is not to refer to its substance or lack of material element, it is to refer to its use and the motive of the user. A cup of cold water is a very physical thing but when it is given to someone in Christ's name it is a spiritual gift (Matt. 10:42). But it is not simply because of creation that the material world has the capacity for spiritual significance. Even more important for Luther is the fact that it was into the fleshly material world that God's Word became incarnate. Jesus, living in the material physical world, has affirmed its significance for all time. To know what God has done we need material things like pages with written words, the physically spoken words of proclamation which make air waves and strike our ears. God certainly can and perhaps does sometimes communicate directly to the hearts of people without coming through any physical means. Luther does not deny it, but he is certain that anything which so comes to someone must be tested for its validity by the objective messages that come through God's material and physical means.

In an earlier chapter we noted that there are at least two connotations of the term "religious experience." The first that comes to mind is an ecstatic, unusual and inner feeling that has the power to persuade a person. A second meaning is that a religious experience is any experience of a person who is religious. In light of the theology of the cross, with its emphasis upon God coming to us in the material everyday world and its call to serve God in that world, it is evident that Luther favors the second understanding of religious experience. The Word comes to us through physical and ordinary means and our daily experiences illuminate its meaning and significance to us. This comes through clearly when Luther says,

> In short he (Paul) calls the entire life of Christians spiritual, in 1 Corinthians 1 and 2. . . . Our fanatics, however, are full of fraud and humbug. They think nothing spiritual can be present where there is anything material and physical, and assert that flesh is of no avail. Actually the opposite is true, The Spirit cannot be with us except in material and physical things such as the Word, water, and Christ's body and in his saints on earth. [32]

When Luther left the monastery to return to the secular world, it symbolized an important theme in his theology. The monastery symbolized a religious place, a triumphalist victory over the temptations of the world. It concentrated on actions directed toward God rather than toward other human beings. Luther's theology of the cross led him to see that God was not to be served in the separated religious place, God was to be served in the world with its people. And just as God is to be served through service to people, so God is best experienced in relationships with other people in the daily life. Christian experience is not simply some inner, mystical, ecstatic feeling; Christian experience is any experience (including hauling manure) of a person who has faith in Christ. Those who would see their inner experiences as more valid, more "spiritual" or more meritorious than the everyday experiences of life simply do not understand the theology of the cross. As God came in the purely human person of Jesus, God continues to come in human experience everywhere.

VI Experience and Liberation Theology

WE HAVE SEEN THAT LUTHER'S THEOLOGY OF THE CROSS led him to see that God's Word comes to us in and through the ordinary events of life. This leads to the understanding that Christian experience includes the everyday experience of Christians in the world. Today there is a major theological movement that emphasizes just this kind of experience. It is the movement that includes the various liberation or political theologies. Today no discussion of experience and Christianity would be complete without a consideration of these theologies.

The theologies of liberation have much to say about the place of experience in Christian faith and understanding but they have not been concerned with those inner forms of experience that have been designated as "religious" in many discussions of experience. Like Luther, these theologies have examined the total life experience of people. They have examined the social, cultural, racial, and economic features of life with a particular concern to examine the contribution to theological thought that can come from out of the experience of the poor, the oppressed, and minority groups. And so, instead of trying to understand Christian faith from the universal experience of humanity as a whole, these theologies have examined Christianity from particular perspectives provided by the experiences of particular groups of human beings.

In 1964 Martin Marty and Dean Peerman began editing a series of books that appeared annually under the general title *New Theology*. Each of these volumes republished articles from the religious journals of the prior year that were deemed to illustrate the major theological trend of that year. The decade during which these books appeared was one of rapid change and upheaval in theology and the editors had no difficulty in finding a different theme for each of their volumes. The ninth volume in the series appeared in 1972 with the theme of "Theology in the Context of the New Particularisms." The editors explained that in the preceding year they had detected a new way of writing theology. It was one which assumes that the language with which theologians work is developed in particular, not universal, communities; that the experiences on the basis of which they do their extrapolating belong to relatively exclusive groups of people; that identity is found when people come to terms with subcommunities before they take on realities like those condensed in the phrase, "the family of man."[1] The result, as the editors noted, was that there were emerging Black Theology, Woman's Theology, Youth theology and the like. Expressing a doubt as to whether this was a wave of the future or a side issue, the editors noted that, at that time, the Bible was being read and theology written in the light of the experience of particular groups.

In fact, the thrust begun by what Marty and Peerman called "new particularisms" has outlived all of the other themes they detected in their decade of watching theological trends. Black liberation theology, for example, has not faded away like so many of the movements of the sixties, but has gone out from the United

States to become an influential international theological movement. Women's theology has continued to develop and has inspired an increasing number of women to take up theological studies.

This move to particularism was regarded as perverse in the traditional strongholds of theology. In the past most theology assumed that its task was to uncover universal truths that applied equally to all people. The glory of Christianity was seen in its universality. Over against the ethnic religion of Judaism, Paul took the gospel to the Gentiles and thus to the whole world. The risen Christ commanded his followers to go into all the world and preach the gospel. Divisions within the church were seen as a great sin but the ecumenical movement of the twentieth century seemed to be overcoming these divisions. In ecumenical discussions, theologians were well on the way towards ridding themselves of denominational particularisms and were making progress in writing what they saw as universal theology. To these theologians the new particularisms seemed like a regressive return to ways that ought to be left behind.

In the confrontation with the new particularisms, the theological establishment has been forced to admit that it has been a homogeneous group and hence particularistic itself. For one thing, theology for the two thousand years of Christianity has been written almost exclusively by males. That means that it has been based, at best, on the experiences of only half of the Christian constituency. But the particularism of the theological establishment goes further than just its maleness. By no means all of the male Christians have been represented in its circles. By and large, it has been the white males of Europe and North America who have written theology. And these white males seldom have come from the exploited or poverty-stricken social classes of their countries. Under the attacks of the new particularisms, it became evident that traditional theology, with its claims to speak for universal human experience, has been based, in reality, on the experience of a small particular group within humanity as a whole.

What has this meant for the development of theology? How has the social, economic, racial, and political experience of the theologians affected or colored their understanding of the faith? Have they really written universal theology for all Christians or have they written theology for the white, male middle and upper classes of the imperialistic nations of the world? In short, just how crucial to the theological endeavor and to religious understanding is the socioeconomic experience of the theologians?

The new particularisms arose because groups of Christians who had not traditionally contributed to the theological scene began to do theology on a major scale in the sixties. Three groups are of special importance. First, there were the theologians of so-called "Third World." These people, coming out of what we had referred to as the North American and European "mission fields," looked at Christian faith from the perspective of their experience as citizens of exploited nations. Second, within North America, the black Christians began to develop "Black Theology" based on the experience of being black in a racist society. Third, an ever-increasing number of women graduating in theological studies began to write theology from out of the experience of being women within a sexist church. Central to all of these groups was a concern to see Christian faith from the perspective of the poor and/or the oppressed. In doing so, they have found that the Bible speaks of liberation in a way that traditional theology has failed to see. Hence the term "liberation theology" can be applied to the work of all of these groups.

What it means to write theology from out of a particular experience of oppression is well illustrated by James Cone's early work, *Black Theology and Black Power*. Contemporary theology seems to agree, says Cone, that the theological task is to bring the gospel to bear on the problems confronted by the present generation. In the United States one problem stands out—the enslavement of black Americans. Nonetheless, contemporary white theologians have been mostly silent about this situation. "There has been no sharp confrontation of the gospel with white racism." [2] To Cone this means that there is a desperate need for a black theology to apply the freeing power of the gospel to the black experience.

For Cone the purpose of a black theology is to ask "What does the Christian gospel have to say to powerless black men whose existence is threatened daily by the insidious tentacles of white power?" [3] Unfortunately, even theologians who were black have not performed this task, says Cone, for they have allowed white theologians to define the theological questions and tasks. Christianity came to the black people through white oppressors and came in a form that required blacks to deny the significance of their blackness. As a result, the black intellectuals have become increasingly suspicious that Christianity is a tool of their oppressors. Thus the question has to be raised as to whether it is possible to affirm one's blackness and still have any identity with the biblical tradition.

When Cone turns to the Scripture with the questions that come from out of black experience he finds that Jesus came to free humanity from the oppressive powers that crush people. He emphasizes Jesus' own definition of his ministry in Jesus' quotation from Isaiah,

> The Spirit of the Lord is upon me, because he has anointed me to preach the good news to the poor. He has sent me to proclaim release to the captives and recovering of sight to the blind, To set at liberty those who are oppressed, To proclaim the acceptable year of the Lord (Luke 4:18-19).

From this and other New Testament passages, Cone concludes that Jesus' work was essentially one of liberation.

It is an age of liberation, in which "the blind receive their sight, the lame walk, the lepers are cleansed, the deaf hear, the dead are raised up, the poor have the good news preached to them" (Luke 7:22). This is not pious talk, and one does not need a seminary degree to interpret the message. It is a message about the ghetto, and all other injustices done in the name of democracy and religion to further the social, political, and economic interests of the oppressor. In Christ, God enters human affairs and takes sides with the oppressed. [4]

Cone concludes that, in the United States today, Christ is in the ghettoes taking the side of the poor and the oppressed. In that situation, "Christianity is not alien to Black Power; it is Black Power." [5]

If the gospel is essentially a word about liberation, the white churches in America are branded as unchristian, claims Cone. As in the early church it became apparent that one could not be both Arian and Christian, likewise in contemporary America it should be apparent that one cannot be both racist and Christian. And yet the white church supported slavery and has been only feeble in its efforts to aid the plight of the black population. It has been more concerned with alcohol or Sunday closing than it has with babies being attacked by rats in the slums. Its theological seminaries only introduced a few black studies when black students forced it on them. Why have the white church and its theologians been so blind to racism, the primary problem of American life? To Cone, it is evident that the church and the theologians have been blinded by their experience which has tied them so close to the structures of a white racist society that they are unable to see how that society contradicts the Christian faith. America has produced no great theologians to compare with the Europeans, in part at least, because its theologians "are too closely tied to the American structure to respond creatively to the life situation of the Church in this society. Instead of seeking to respond to the problems which are unique to this country, most Americans look to Europe for the newest word worth theologizing about." [6] In short, the white American experience has made it impossible for white theologians to see how the gospel applies to the major problem of American life.

On the other hand, Cone believes that black theologians can see what white theologians have missed. This is not because he claims that black theologians are more wise or virtuous than the white theologians: they can see it because their experience has been different. They have seen life and hence come to Christianity from the experience of being an oppressed and exploited people. The black people of America have known slavery from the point of view of slaves. White Christians, knowing slavery from the point of view of the masters, could rationalize slavery and find ways of reconciling it to Christianity. The black church, however, born in slavery, could not "accept white interpretations of Christianity, which suggested the gospel was concerned with freedom of the soul and not the body." [7] Black preachers found themselves in "a state of existential absurdity." "They could not understand why God even permitted slavery." [8] And so from the beginning the black church was open to hear the liberating message of Scripture which had fallen upon the deaf ears of the white church.

A theme similar to Cone's runs through the various currents of liberation and political theologies. The two terms, "liberation" and "political" describe quite similar movements in contemporary theology. This is illustrated by Dorothee Soelle who is known as a leading exponent of political theology. When, however, she spoke at a conference on political theology at the University of Saskatchewan, the theme of her address was "Liberation." At the same time, liberation theologians make it clear that their theology is meant to have political consequences. These theologies are written from out of the experience of oppression.

As Cone writes from the experience of being black in a racist society, women write from the experience of being women in a sexist society and third world theologians write from the experience of being oppressed under colonialism. Liberation theology, therefore, is concerned with oppression and is dedicated to political means for removing the oppression.

The liberation theologies that have arisen in the Third World have often drawn on the writing of Karl Marx as an aid to analyzing their colonial experience. Gustavo Gutierrez, one of the founders of liberation theology in South America, has said that theology in that continent must use Marx because the people are already thinking in Marxian terms.

A concept taken from Marx by liberation theologies is that of "ideology." Although this term is used to describe a number of different themes, a basic one is that all thinking is conditioned or even determined by the material socioeconomic base of life. This means that thinkers who believe that they are simply following the objective evidence toward the truth are, in fact, often rationalizing the interests of their particular social classes. As Cone charges that white Christians have written their theologies so that they support the status of the dominant race, so Third World theologians charge that traditional theology has supported colonialism. Theologians spun beautiful theological justifications for going into the Third World countries but the result was the exploitation of the native peoples by the colonial powers. Women likewise argue that theology written by males has defended male supremacy.

One of the reasons for using the term "political theology" is to draw attention to the fact that all theology is written from a particular political bias. As Alfredo Fierro puts it, "Every theology is conditioned by socioeconomic factors and realities. Today's political theology enjoys one advantage over previous theologies: it is consciously aware of that fact."[9]

An ideology is dangerous when it is not recognized. Persons are convinced that they are striving after the truth, the whole truth and nothing but the truth, but, in fact, all the time their sociopolitical interest is distorting the results that they obtain. This is illustrated by Dorothee Soelle who challenges the thesis of existentialist Rudolf Bultmann when he says that "The meaning of history always lies in the present." She says, "In the face of such a statement, we have no right to disregard the interest that produced it, which means concretely that we must raise the questions posed by Karl Marx. Whose interest is served by perceiving the meaning of history always in the present?"[10] It seems obvious to Soelle that the poor and wretched of the earth do not talk or think this way. This statement can only come from one whose present situation is relatively satisfying and comfortable. The poor and oppressed will inevitably seek the meaning of history somewhere else than in the present. In particular, they will seek history's meaning in a more desirable future.

Some Marxian theorists have interpreted the effects of socio-economic conditioning in a deterministic fashion although it is doubtful that Marx himself did. At any rate, most of the liberation theologians do not interpret it deterministically. They believe that once theology is aware that all thinking is done from a particular class perspective, it is possible to make a conscious choice as to which class one will espouse. To liberation theologians, it is obvious that the Bible takes the side of the poor and oppressed in any social situation. The center of the Old Testament is the Exodus which was the freeing of a people from slavery. Throughout the Old Testament a central theme of the prophets is to condemn the rich and powerful who exploit the poor and to call for justice (e.g. Amos, 4:1-3; Micah 2:1-5; Isa. 1:16-17; Jer. 22:13-19; Hos. 4:1-2). In the New Testament, as we have seen, Jesus defined his ministry in terms of good news for the poor and liberation for captives. He consciously drew in the poor, the oppressed and the outcasts of his society. In a parable of the last judgment, Jesus pictured judgment as based solely on the response to the needs of the hungry, the sick and the imprisoned (Matt. 25:31-46). If, then, all theology is done from a class perspective, liberation theologies affirm that we can only be true to the Scriptures by doing theology from the perspective of the poor and the oppressed.

In an earlier chapter we saw that Luther warned that the inner religious experiences of a person were subject to sin. The spirit whom a person experienced was all too often the spirit that one wanted to experience. Thus Luther saw the need to test all such experiences by the objective word of Scripture. Liberation theology's discussion of ideology helps us to see the dynamics involved in Luther's point. Before a person has an inner religious experience, there have been the years of conditioning within a particular socioeconomic class. Inevitably this class experience will condition a person to see life from the point of view of that class. An inner personal experience is unlikely to cause a person to look critically on the values and viewpoints of his or her class. It is more likely that the experience will simply reinforce the basic class perspectives, giving them a divine sanction.

We are able to see today that ideology does not arise only from the conditioning of one's socioeconomic class, it also arises from sex roles. The rise of the women's movement in theology has forced us to see that past theology has operated with an ideology of sex as well as of class. The predominantly male theologians have presented us with a male God and a male understanding of the gospel itself. For centuries male theologians have unashamedly spoken about the "Doctrine of Man" and referred to God exclusively with masculine pronouns. If challenged (and they were not often challenged over the years) they would have responded that "man" is a generic term that of course includes women and that everyone knows that God is beyond being male or female.

But today women's theology is forcing us to ask if the male terminology was as benign as the male theologians would have us believe. So long as the church was content with a God who was pictured as male and its theology has reflected male experience, the males have dominated the life of the church. Furthermore women's inferior place within the church has been used to justify the oppression of women in the wider society. All of this could be seen fully only when women, finally refusing to be simply imitators of male theology, began to study the Bible and Christian faith from out of the perspective of their experience as women. The result has been a number of insights into the nature of Christian faith.

An example of this is the work of Phyllis Trible, an Old Testament scholar. She begins her book, *God and the Rhetoric of Sexuality* by noting that certain biblical passages reappear in different settings. When this happens the original meaning often is changed and even sometimes contradicted. She concludes that "Scripture in itself yields multiple interpretations of itself." [11] These different interpretations arise from the attempt of the writers to bring the biblical message into a vital relationship with the context and experience of the interpreter. Following this clue, she sets herself the task of interpreting Scripture in light of the contemporary feminist critique of culture.

Trible finds a justification for her task in Genesis 1:27 where we read,

> And God created humankind in his image,
> in the image of God created he him:
> male and female created he them.

Analyzing this text, Trible finds that it is as male and female that humankind is in the image of God. From this she concludes that both male and female metaphors are needed if we are to speak of God. Metaphors which refer to God as father or husband are only partial metaphors as are those which refer to God as pregnant woman and mother. Thus the text "presents an equality in the image of God male *and* female, although the Bible overwhelmingly favors male metaphors for deity."[12] This gives Trible justification for investigating female metaphors for God in the Scriptures.

One such metaphor which Trible finds is the Hebrew word, *rahamim* which she follows through several biblical passages. The root of the term is in *rehem* which means "womb" and *rahamim* means literally the compassion of the mother's womb for her child. Such motherly love is seen as a uniquely pure form of love and the term is applied widely in the Old Testament to describe God's love for the people. This female metaphor has, by and large, been lost in most translations of the Scripture. For example, Jeremiah 31:20 (c) is translated rather literally by Trible to read,

> Therefore, my womb trembles for him;
> I will truly show motherly-compassion upon him.
> Oracle of Yahweh.

However, in the RSV the same lines are translated,

> Therefore my heart yearns for him;
> I will surely have mercy on him
> says the Lord.

It is obvious that the latter translation has hidden all female elements in the metaphor of God's love.

Trible summarizes her following of the word *rahamim* through many passages by saying,

> With persistence and power the root *rhm* journeys throughout the traditions of Israel to establish a major metaphor for biblical faith: semantic movement from the wombs of women to the compassion of God. Though readers of the Old Testament have

often been slow to perceive this speech, they have long been recipients of its manifold blessings. For us the language has unfolded new dimensions of the image of God male *and* female. [13]

Trible is not working with a new discovery about the root meanings of *rahamim*. Old Testament scholars have no doubt always known this. But Trible has analyzed the significance of this motherly image of God in a way that has not been done before. We are forced to ask whether this is because almost all of the Old Testament scholars through the centuries have been males who have read the Bible from out of male experience whereas Trible is reading it from out of her female experience.

Trible further illustrates the importance of a female perspective in a later chapter on the story of Adam and Eve. She notes that male interpreters have long used this story to justify male superiority and female inferiority as the will of God. Over against this, her careful exegesis demonstrates that the story pictures an equality of male and female in God's sight and in God's plan for humankind.

For example, when Eve is created, the traditional translations have described her as Adam's "helper" or "help meet" (Gen. 2:18-20). These terms imply a subordination of Eve to Adam. But, Trible points out, the Hebrew word that is used here, *ezer,* has no such connotations of inferior status. On the contrary, in the Hebrew Scriptures it is often used to describe God. It would be better to translate it as "companion" so that the equality of Adam and Eve in the original story is brought out. It is only after the temptation and fall that Adam is made the master over Eve (Gen. 3:16). But this is not simply a distortion of woman's created role as companion, it is also a distortion of man's role when he becomes the master. He too has been divorced from the mutuality of man and woman which he celebrated in his words, "This at last is bone of my bones and flesh of my flesh" (Gen.

2:23). The implication is clear that, if there is to be salvation, it must free woman from the penalty of being subjected and man from the penalty of being a master.

These various particularistic theologies raise important questions for the future of theology. Never again can we pretend that our theologizing is a pure and simple search for the truth. To be human means that we do read the Bible from out of the experiences we have had. What the Bible can say to us depends on what we can hear and what we can hear depends on the experience of life that we have had. But what conclusion should we draw from this? Is it good enough to be unashamedly particularistic? Must each particular group or subgroup have its own particular theology with no hope of real communication between the groups? Are white people to worship a white God and a white Jesus while black people worship a black God and a black Jesus? And will other races have to have corresponding colors for their God and Christ? Are male Christians to worship God the Father while female Christians worship God the Mother? James Cone says, "First, there can be no theology of the gospel which does not arise from an oppressed community. This is so because God in Christ has revealed himself as a God whose righteousness is inseparable from the weak and helpless in human society." [14] Does this mean that once a group is delivered from oppression, it can no longer develop a theology? If all groups are liberated, will all theology disappear? Behind all of these questions lies the basic question whether our particular racial, sexual, economic, and political experience predetermines what theology we are able to produce, accept or understand. In the next chapter we shall turn to the themes of particularism and universalism in the Bible to see if we can find some answers to these questions.

VII Particularism and Universalism in the Bible

IN THE PRECEDING CHAPTER we saw that the rise of the new particularisms was disturbing to traditional theology which believed that its task was to produce universal truths. When, however, we turn to the Bible we find that particularism is not as foreign to its message as traditional theology would have led us to believe. Marty and Peerman, in their volume on particularism, suggest that the movement from universalism to particularism can be seen as a movement from a Greek philosophical mode of thought to a Hebrew biblical mode of thinking. There is much to support this suggestion.

Much of Greek philosophy scorned the concrete and empirical. It sought to find "timeless" truths which, being equally true everywhere and always, are unaffected by the passage of time or by anything that happens in human history. Thus mathematics was the great symbol of truth to these Greeks. The angles at the base of an isosceles triangle are everywhere and always equal. Such timeless truths, the Greeks believed, were made in heaven and when we human creatures learn them, we are related to heaven and eternity. When, however, we try to transpose these timeless truths into the realm of space and time, they lose some of their divinity and eternal nature. Whenever we try to draw an isosceles triangle, it is inevitably imperfect and, in fact, the angles at its base are never quite equal. Within space and time, the Greeks believed, we cannot hope to have more than a pale image of the heavenly truths. Truth, therefore, must be sought through the unchanging ways of pure mind and pure logic. Truth is found only to the degree that we escape from this finite changing world of space and time.

This Greek philosophy has had a great influence on Christian thought through the centuries. A much-loved Christian hymn shows the influence of this point of view.

> Change and decay in all around I see
> O thou who changest not, abide with me.

This hymn expresses the Greek view that in the world of change the truth cannot be found. Truth is only found by looking to the changeless God who is apart from this changing world. For the Greeks this meant that God had to be found in "spiritual ways"—mystical illumination, or pure logic. This implies that God is equally knowable in every time and place by any person who puts forth the necessary effort. This Greek influence is, in large part, responsible for the idea that Christian theology should consist of timeless universal truths which can be known equally well anywhere or at any time by those who objectively put their minds to finding them.

Nothing could be more different from this than the Hebraic-biblical way of thinking. The Hebrews found God speaking to them precisely in and through the vicissitudes of historical time. Yahweh called Abraham and his descendants to be a chosen covenant people and it was in the history of this particular people that Yahweh was revealed. Once when I was teaching a seminar on the "Idea of God in Western Thought," we had studied Plato and Aristotle and then turned to the Old Testament. One of the more perceptive students said, "Now I see the difference between Greek and Hebrew thought. Aristotle knew that there was a God because pure objective logic led him to see that there always has to be a First Cause. The Hebrews knew that there was a God because God delivered them from Egypt." That is a good summary of the two modes of thinking. The Greek philosophical mode of thought looked for truths that would be equally evident to any rational person anywhere or anytime who engages in pure thought. But the God of the Exodus can be known only by looking at particular events in time. Yahweh is known only where and when Yahweh wills to be known.

In the New Testament this Hebraic thought is even more evident. In the Old Testament God was revealed in and through the history of a particular people. In the New Testament the revelation of God centers down to one particular person. In Jesus Christ the Word became flesh and dwelt among us. To those who think in the Greek philosophical mode, it will always be a scandal to claim that truth of such an ultimate nature is to be found within the relativities of historical existence.

In John's Gospel Jesus says, "I am the way, and the truth, and the life" (John 14:6). To a Greek philosopher, or to most modern philosophers, this seems a nonsensical statement. A proposition, a system of thought or a belief may be true but what does it mean to say that a person, a living, breathing human being is the truth? The point is that Jesus is here not portraying truth as an abstract theory or as something timeless such as the proposition that two plus two equals four. Of course such truths have their place. But Jesus is pointing to another kind of truth. This kind of truth, says Jesus, is something that happens, truth is lived, it appears in time and history, it takes on a concrete and particular form. To know such truth we do not engage in objective reasoning, we must know the person who embodies it.

If we take the Greek point of view, truth is seen as a whole, eternally the same. Therefore, in principle it is possible to see all of the truth at any time. In fact, of course, it is recognized that considerable time may elapse before the whole of a system of truth is discovered, but that is because the human mind is weak and slow and often distracted by other matters. Nonetheless, the frailty of the human mind does not change the fact that the truth was there all the time and could have been discovered sooner. The truths of geometry did not become true when Euclid discovered them. They always had been true and it is only accidental that it was Euclid, in his time, who discovered them rather than someone else in some other time and place.

It is different when we look at Hebraic thought. For the Hebrews, God's truth is not available all at once for any person who may strive to discover it. God came to Abraham and made a covenant with him and his descendants. Abraham was still, however, a long way from the whole truth. Abraham, we read, went forth in faith, not knowing where he was to go (Heb. 11:8). He went in faith precisely because the whole of God's truth had not been given to him. He had a promise which could only be confirmed and fulfilled with the passage of time. Centuries later Moses received the Ten Commandments and the rest of the law, but these were not the complete truth. There was still the promised land which Moses was allowed to view only from afar. When the covenant people got to the promised land there was still much to be revealed to them. Their prophets unfolded to them the meaning of what had happened. Their deliverance from slavery called them to live in righteousness and justice. They had to learn that there was more to the promised land than a change in geography. From Amos they had to learn of God's justice and from Hosea they were to learn of God's mercy. But still the picture was not complete and the promise came that God would send a Messiah. Who and what the Messiah would be could not be known until he had come. The tragedy according to the New Testament is that the people of the promise did not recognize the Messiah. He was not the kind of Messiah for which they were looking.

In short, for the Bible, God's truth is not dropped from heaven all in one piece because it is not the timeless kind of truth for which the Greeks were seeking. God's truth is made known through a long process that occurs within time. It is claimed that the Koran existed in heaven from eternity and an angel dictated it to Mohammad who recorded it word for word. The Hebrew Scripture makes no such claim for itself. It is made up from the materials of human history. The Christian practice of dividing the Bible into the Old Covenant and the New Covenant symbolizes how the biblical truth developed. This occurred because the biblical faith is based on revelation; its truth is not discoverable by human effort. It is given in God's good time.

Another distinction between Greek philosophical and Hebraic ways of thinking now appears. Greek views of the truth always go with elitism. Although, in theory, the truth can be discovered by anyone, in fact it is always recognized that it is an elite few who are able to discover it. Plato taught that the nations of the world could never be delivered from their evils until they had philosophers for their kings. The philosophers were the elite few who could see the whole of truth. Even the limited democracies of the Greek city-states were seen as dangerous by Plato because they put power in the hands of the uncouth and unenlightened masses. On the other hand, biblical revelation is seen as coming particularly to the poor and disadvantaged. It is always surprising to see the ones to whom God is revealed: a drifting nomad like Abraham, a cowardly Moses or a Galilean carpenter with no place to lay his head.

An interesting illustration of this is the place that women play in receiving revelation. Although the Bible arose from out of a patriarchical culture which relegated women to a subordinate position, God often chose women to play a key role. Sarah certainly learned as much of God's revelation as her husband, Abraham, and on occasion it was she, rather than Abraham who understood what God was saying (e.g. Gen. 21:12). Moses was only around to receive the Ten Commandments because God had first worked through his mother and sister to preserve his life. Mary, the mother of Jesus proclaimed the Magnificat in which she marvelled that God had chosen one of her low estate (Luke 1:47-55). Women had an important role in Jesus' mission and it was no accident that they were the first ones to witness his resurrection.

Paul sums up the place of the poor and humble in God's revelation when he describes the early Christians. He says, "not many of you were wise according to worldly standards, not many were powerful, not many were of noble birth" (1 Cor. 1:26).

Although the Bible presents a view of truth that is quite different from that of Greek philosophers, when Christianity spread into the Graeco-Roman world, minds trained in the Greek method of thought began to interpret it. That was necessary and good but it did create problems. One of these was a tendency to assume that, despite the developmental nature of truth within the Bible, now that we have the Bible it provides our timeless truths. There can be no further revelation or new understanding. Where the Bible has spoken, the case is closed. And so frequently in Christian history the Bible has been treated as the final word on such things as astronomy, biology, marriage and divorce, homosexuality, slavery, the status of women and so on. Despite the fact that the scriptural statements involved were spoken in and to a particular time and place, they are now viewed as timeless truths to be applied in the same way to all times and places.

This view that the Scripture provides timeless truths is not only contrary to the way revelation develops in the Bible, it is contrary to the teaching of Jesus. In John's Gospel, Jesus says, "I have much more to tell you, but now it would be too much for you to bear. But when the Spirit of truth comes, he will lead you into all the truth" (John 16:12-13 TEV). Here is the definite promise that God, through the Spirit, will continue to guide the church into further truth. God will continue to act and speak in and through history. When the Bible is treated as a collection of timeless truths, it distorts the biblical view that its ultimate truth is a person and allegiance to the truth is allegiance to Christ. The search for timeless truths puts allegiance to propositions and doctrines in place of allegiance to Christ.

But the thrust of biblical faith has been too strong to be stifled permanently by the Greek view of truth. The Christian church has again and again been reminded that Christ is the truth and Christian faith means loyalty to Christ. As a result, in the light of new experience, it has been able to follow Christ into new paths. Although impatient Christians often feel that the church is frozen into a conservative worship of the past, a view of the church's history shows that it has been remarkably flexible in adopting to new experiences of life. In fact, this may be one advantage Christianity has had over other major world religions: because other religions are often wed to timeless and unchanging truths, they have found difficulty in adapting to the changing experiences of history. Because Christians have realized that their ultimate truth is a person, they have been able to transcend their traditions and find new ways to be loyal to Christ in new situations.

An example of Christianity's ability to change is found in the question of slavery. Nowhere in the New Testament is slavery explicitly condemned. On the contrary, the New Testament writers frequently admonish the slaves to be obedient to their masters (e.g. Col. 3:22; Titus 2:9). Paul returned the runaway slave, Onesimus, to his master, Philemon (Philemon 1:1-25).

Christians who saw the Bible as a collection of timeless truths to be applied in the same way to all times and places used these texts to justify the continuance of slavery. Also, the argument was made that slavery was part of the order of creation and hence always to be in existence among human beings.

In the eighteenth and nineteenth centuries, for reasons too complex to analyze here, a widespread debate arose over the question of slavery. A growing number of Christians refused to see the biblical references to slavery as timeless truths that would make slavery a permanent condition of human beings. As Christians experienced the reality of slavery in light of their loyalty to Christ, they found a contradiction. Christ came with love for all people, he saw each human so precious in God's eyes that the hairs of each person's head were numbered. Christ, who gave his life a ransom for many, announced that his mission was to release prisoners and liberate captives while proclaiming good news to the poor. How could this Christ be reconciled with the practice of buying, selling, and working human beings like lesser animals? And so many Christian became increasingly convinced that slavery was evil.

How then did such Christians handle the clear statements of Scripture telling slaves to obey their masters, etc.? These came to be seen as statements made to the particular situation in which they were written and not to be taken as commandments for all times and places. Given the situation of Christians as a small persecuted minority in the Roman Empire, there was no hope of overthrowing slavery. If Christian slaves were disobedient to their masters, this would not help to overthrow slavery, rather it would only be another excuse for persecuting all Christians. Furthermore, the New Testament writers obviously believed that the Second Coming of Christ was imminent and so slaves could wait for Christ to set them free. If Paul could even advise against getting married in light of the imminent end (1 Cor. 7:25-26), it is not strange that he advised slaves to bear their lot for the short time left. By the eighteenth century, however, Christians were not a powerless minority but, in many countries, a powerful majority who could abolish slavery. No longer was the second coming seen as imminent, rather the experience of nineteen hundred years had taught Christians that they were to accept the responsibility of an indefinite future. And finally, a few daring Christians at that time were prepared to say that slavery was one of those questions on which Peter and Paul did not have the whole truth. The evil of slavery was one of those truths which Jesus had promised would be revealed by the Holy Spirit at a later time.

Here it is important to be clear as to what is being said. Christians have always recognized that Christ is the final and complete revelation. In fact, recognizing this is an important part of the definition of being a Christian. So the argument here is not that we should seek a further revelation beyond Jesus, but that Jesus is not dead and buried, he is the risen Lord, dwelling in a living body, the church. Therefore, there is no end to the growth in the understanding of what Christ means for life and the world. Particularly, as the world changes, Christ will bring new insights to the church to meet the changing times.

Christians who have held to a view of timeless truths have often quoted Hebrews 13:8 which reads "Jesus Christ is the same yesterday and today and forever." However, what this verse says is that it is *Jesus Christ* who is the same, not truths, not even truths about Jesus. Furthermore, if Jesus Christ is the same yesterday, today and forever, it means that he today is the one who is still calling us to change, to newness. He is still telling us that we cannot sew new patches on old garments or put new wine into old wine skins (Matt. 9:16-17). He is still speaking to the concrete needs of people.

Paradoxical as it may appear at first, what is being said here is, in essence, what the Reformers said in their phrase *sola scriptura* (the Scriptures alone.) It is paradoxical because in the contemporary world that slogan has all too often been used to defend a timeless-truth approach to Scripture. The Reformers used *sola scriptura,* however, to oppose the view of the medieval church which put tradition on par with Scripture. The result of this, Protestants argued, was to freeze the interpretation of Scriptures. Tradition was the way in which those who came before had heard the Scripture speaking to them. When this was put on par with Scripture, it denied those in the present the opportunity to go to the Scriptures and to hear what the Scriptures would say to them.

This interpretation of the Reformers is illustrated in the Lutheran Confessions. The strongest statement of the *sola scriptura* position is made in The Formula of Concord, Part I. The Formula begins by affirming that the Old and New Testaments "are the only rule and norm according to which all doctrines and teachers alike must be appraised and judged. . . ." [1] It then goes on to say that other writings of ancient and modern persons, "whatever their names," must be subordinated to the Scriptures. What we can see in such writings is a witness "to the fashion in which the doctrine of the prophets and apostles was preserved in post-apostolic times." [2] In short, earlier interpretations of the Scripture are to be held in respect. We can learn from them, but they are never to prevent Christians from going to the Scriptures to hear what Christ is saying to their time and place.

This principle of the Lutheran Confessions is illustrated in practice in the Augsburg Confession, Article XXVIII. In a discussion of the power of the bishops to legislate practice in the church, the confessors refer to 1 Cor. 11:2-10. In this passage Paul directed that women should cover their heads in public worship. Paul justified this directive by a long discourse that argued that practice was required by the orders of the creation. To any who believed in the Bible as a set of timeless truths this would be a conclusive command for all times and places. This was how it had been interpreted in the medieval church. But the Augsburg Confession clearly refutes this interpretation for the contemporary situation saying, ". . . no one would say that a woman commits a sin if without offense to others she goes out with uncovered head."[3] Here the Reformers illustrate that the *sola scriptura* principle means that Christ must be free to speak to the contemporary situation. What was commanded in another time and place may not be binding upon our time and place.

This quick survey of the Bible and the Reformers' interpretation of it, gives a strong basis for the particularistic interpretations. Since biblical revelation came to particular people in particular times and places, today it seems justified that people respond to God's Word from out of their particular historical experience. As Karl Barth put it, God does not call station to station, God calls person to person. Therefore, James Cone is correct in trying to hear what God is saying to the ghetto and Phyllis Trible is correct in listening to hear the meaning of God's Word for women today. Liberation theology is in harmony with Scripture when it does not treat the Bible as a message "to whom it may concern" but as a direct address to the poor and oppressed of today and to Third World people suffering from colonialism.

There is much in the Bible to justify the particularist approach but particularism is not the whole story of the Bible. At the very time when Abraham and his descendants are called and particularism is instituted, God gives the chosen people a goal—that all the peoples of the world may be blessed (Gen. 12:3). Throughout its history, the people of God have been tempted to forget that goal and to assume that to be chosen was to be given special favors from God. But the Old Testament prophets would not let them get away with such views. On the contrary, because they alone of all peoples had been chosen, they would be punished for *all* of their sins (Amos 3:2). The implication is clear that the other people, not having the privileges of the covenant people, would not be held responsible for all of their sins. Again and again the prophets reminded the covenant people that the purpose of their covenant was that all nations might come to worship the God of Abraham, Isaac, and Jacob (e.g. Isa. 2:2-3). And so, even in the highly particularistic Old Testament, the final vision and goal is a universal one.

In the New Testament this universalism comes out more clearly. The risen Christ commands his followers to go into the whole world with the Gospel (Matt. 28:19). Paul fights and wins the battle to free the church from the idea that converts to Christ have to become practicing Jews (Acts 15:1-11). The book of Acts is the story of the church moving out into the whole known world of its time. The basic message of the New Testament is that God so loved the *world* (not just Jews or Christians) that the Messiah was given (John 3:16). From all of this Paul can conclude that in Christ there is neither Jew nor Gentile, slave or free, male or female (Gal. 3:28).

In light of the contemporary emphasis on particular experience, especially the particular socioeconomic experience, what does it mean that the Bible provides us with both particularistic and universal themes? Certainly it means that the universalism of the Bible is not the universalism of timeless truths as in Greek thought. It is a universalism that begins with particular people in a particular time and place. Although all the nations are called to worship Yahweh, they are never allowed to forget that Yahweh is the God of Abraham, Isaac, and Jacob; the God who came to a particular people. But the Word that comes to particular people is never simply meant for them alone. It is a Word that is to be brought to all people.

Because the biblical Word does come to particular people, what is heard will depend on the experience of those to whom the

Word comes. Inevitably, we tend to interpret any text in light of our own experience. Often what a text can say to us depends on the questions we put to it. And our questions arise from out of our life experiences—social, economic, political, racial, sexual and so on. This is the truth that the particularistic theologies are expressing for us.

The rise of liberation theology itself illustrates this truth. So long as theology was done primarily by white, male, middle class theologians from the Western world, the biblical theme of liberation did not stand out with prominence. After all, such theologians were not primarily concerned with being liberated and so they did not come to the Scriptures with that question in mind. The many references to liberation in the Bible were usually interpreted in terms of the individual and individual sin.

The terms "redeemer, redemption, redeem etc." are frequently used in the Bible. Traditionally theology came to see these terms as having a spiritual significance related to the life of individuals and their particular sins. Nonetheless, the terms were not primarily religious terms in biblical times, they were sociopolitical terms. When persons were captured and held for ransom by brigands or enemies in war, a redemption price had to be paid for their release. Slaves could be freed from slavery when a redemption price was paid for them. In each case the person paying the redemption price was referred to as the redeemer. In the Old Testament, these terms are most often used in Second Isaiah. F.J. Taylor says that when Second Isaiah uses the term "redeemer" for God, "The primary reference is to the exercise of that divine right and power for the people . . . by which the poor and feeble exilic community is to be restored to its rightful land." [4] It is obvious that today we would get much closer to the biblical meaning of these terms if we translated them by the terms "liberator," "liberation," "liberate," etc. Terms based on "redeem" have taken on connotations of individualism and have been so spiritualized that the original sociopolitical references are lost.

It was when theology began to be done by people who were blacks, citizens of Third World countries and women that the biblical concern with liberation began to be emphasized. God, these people noted, did not just redeem individuals from their sins, God liberated the whole people from their slavery in Egypt. The significance of this emphasis on liberation was apparent to these theologians because their life-experience had sharpened their eyes to see references to liberation. Because each of us tends to come to Scripture with our own questions and concerns, it is not surprising that the theme of liberation has been emphasized in a wholly new way by theologians who come from the poor and/or oppressed groups. But, having made this discovery, they are able to demonstrate to others that this is a Word of Scripture to all of us. And so the biblical particularism does not mean that we all must go off into our private corners to listen for Christ's word to us alone. It does not mean that we are predetermined by our socioeconomic or political experience to see only one set of meanings in the Bible. It does mean that each of us, having first heard the Word speak to our particular experience, can share with and learn from the others who have also first heard the Word speaking to their experience.

Paul's analogy of the church as the body of Christ is helpful at this point (1 Cor. 12:12-31). Just as the hand cannot say that it has no need for the foot, or vice versa, so in the church of Christ, each of the particularistic understandings of the Scripture is needed. Each of them is able to throw its particular light on the gospel. This means that we should not move too quickly to do our theological thinking from the point of view of humanity as such. First we have to understand what the Word says to us in our particular experience.

This theme is illustrated in the rise of black power and black theology. The black race came to see that premature integration would mean the loss of all the distinctiveness of the black race unless it had first developed a clear appreciation of its own uniqueness. And so the themes of "black power" or "black is beautiful" had to be developed. In the same way, before the black church can make its full contribution in the body of Christ, it must develop a black theology which witnesses to how the gospel has spoken to its uniqueness.

But, as the goal of God's covenant with the Jews was that all the people should find a blessing, so the insights of black theology should lead to the liberation of all people. Racism is not only a curse to the exploited race, it is also a curse to the exploiters. Liberation for blacks will be a liberation for the whites who have exploited them. In the last chapter we saw that the Fall distorted the role of both men and women when men came to rule over women. Liberation of women, therefore, not only liberates women from the curse of being subjugated, it also liberates men from the role of masters and frees both men and women for the mutuality between them that was intended by God in creation. Liberation of the Third World colonies will be liberation for the imperialistic powers of the First World.

From the foregoing we can conclude that it is necessary that we develop our particular theologies, based upon our particular experiences. But, as Peerman and Marty pointed out, it is also dangerous. [5]

Particularism is dangerous, in the first place, because it is always tempting to think that the gospel as interpreted in the light of a particular experience is the truth, the whole truth, and nothing but the truth. But we are all finite and our experiences are finite and none of us can see the fullness of the gospel's meaning. We need to listen to each other. The particularism of traditional theology, which we have recognized, illustrates how easy it is to assume that our particular experience is the true experience of humanity as such. But none of the new particularisms will be exempt from this temptation. It would be easy to glean quotations from representatives of the new particularisms where the assumption is revealed that this particular group has a monopoly on the insights of God's revelation. At present I am living in Canada and Canadian particularism has been greatly emphasized in recent years. In the Canadian church we hear pleas to develop a "Canadian theology." This is right, good and necessary. But I have often heard students complain because they have to study the theology of non-Canadians such as Barth, Tillich, Moltmann and Cone. If our Canadian particularism blinds us to the insights to be gained from non-Canadian theology, our Canadian theology will be a curse and not a blessing.

A second danger of particularism is that it may blunt our understanding of the radical love of God. Political-liberation theologies tell us that all theology is done from a class bias and therefore we must choose to do theology from the point of view of the poor and oppressed classes. This is a half truth. Where there is oppression, Christians are called by their faith to oppose the oppression and to take the side of the oppressed. A Christianity that can sanction exploitation and oppression is indeed heretical. But that is not the final word. Christ died for the oppressors as well as the oppressed. Beyond the battle for justice lies God's acceptance of sinners. This was illustrated by Karl Barth's relationship to Nazism. No theologian opposed Nazism more consistently than Barth. He called the nations of the world to oppose it and gave theological sanction to the war against Nazism. But even as the end of the war was in sight, Barth began to speak out with a concern for the German people. He declared that God's love was offered to the Nazis too, to the S.S. and the German Youth etc. These were difficult words for the Allied Nations to hear at that time but they were certainly words that a Christian theology needed to speak. And so today, while God calls us to deliver the oppressed from their oppression, God also calls us to love the oppressors for whom Christ died. Of course, Christian love for them implies that they need to be delivered from their roles as oppressors. Oppressors can be liberated from their state only when the oppressed are liberated, but Christians must be concerned for both oppressed and oppressor.

Our brief look at the particularisms of liberation theology has revealed another dimension to the concept of experience. It is a truncated view of religious experience if we think of it simply as the inner experience of individuals. We do not live in a vacuum. Our understanding of God's revelation and our inner experience of God will inevitably be colored by our experience in society. Perhaps, in the last analysis, the sin against the Holy Spirit that is unforgivable is the sin of assuming that our particular interpretation of God's Word, based on our particular experience, has exhausted the message that God has to speak.

VIII   Conclusion

We began our study by observing that this is a time when inner experience holds a central place in North American religion. This phenomenon caused us to ask about the place experience ought to have in the Christian life. As we pursued the subject through a philosophical analysis of experience, Luther's views and liberation theologies, we found two basic questions emerging. The first is, what experiences are to be seen as Christian experience? Do we mean simply an inner "mystical" personal experience or do we mean any experience of a person who is a Christian? The second question asks what is the authority of experience in Christianity? Is experience a sufficient basis for confirming, criticizing or changing the beliefs and practices of Christians and the church? Is experience the basis for personal assurance of salvation? In this chapter we shall draw conclusions about these questions.

When first we speak of religious or Christian experience, it is usually assumed that we are speaking of inner personal experiences that are of an unusual and ecstatic nature. There is no question but that such inner experiences are universal to the human race and are part of all the world's religions. Christian experience certainly includes such experiences. Our study, however, suggests that there is a wider group of experiences that need to be included in any consideration of Christian experience.

Luther's theology of the cross supported the thesis that any experience may be seen as Christian experience by the Christian. A theology of the cross recognizes that we do not see God face to face in this life. God is always mediated to us through persons, things and events of life in the world. The belief that God is known more clearly in inner experience because that is more "spiritual" is seen as a form of triumphalism that believes that in the inner life there is a more pure, less material, presentation of God. The Christian view, however, is that the material world is God's good creation and the biblical God communicates through the mundane events of human history.

This theme is illustrated in the contemporary liberation theologies. These theologies affirm that the most significant experiences for Christian understanding are the experiences found in the socioeconomic life of people. Liberation theologies believe that the meaning Christianity will have for us will depend on the particular group, social class, sex or race through which we have experienced life.

Probably there would be few today who would give an either/ or answer to the question of what experiences may be Christian. Almost all Christians would agree that God may be met both in the everyday experiences of life and in inner personal experiences. The real debates are those about the relative importance of these experiences. Most of the groups that Luther criticized continued to use the bread, wine and water of the sacraments. What concerned Luther was that they did not see them as being of primary importance. For them it was the Holy Spirit, identified with the inner experience, that really mattered. Those who had been baptized by the Holy Spirit, and only those, could profit from the baptism by water. Similarly today we are told by some Christians that it is only the person who has been born again through an inner experience who is in the position to see Christian significance in the everyday events of life. This inner experience is the primary and crucial matter; everyday experience is secondary. On the other hand, many liberation theologians see the socioeconomic experience as decisive for thought. Without denying that Christians have inner personal experiences, they argue that the interpretation of such experiences is always predetermined by one's experience in the socioeconomic sphere. Inner experiences are incapable of remolding the values and lifestyle that have been absorbed from a person's place in the social structures.

If one takes the position that any experience of a Christian may be a Christian experience, depending on the interpretation, it follows that we cannot claim a higher priority for either inner experiences or for external ones. Behind the claim for the priority of the inner experience lies the dualistic view of the world which believes that the non-material spirituality is superior to that where matter is involved. From this it is inferred that the Holy Spirit operates only in a nonmaterial way. This idea has been encouraged by the wide use of the term "Holy Ghost" for the Holy Spirit. When this usage first developed, "ghost" did not have its modern connotations. But today a ghost is what is left of a person when all the material body has been removed. The term Holy Ghost thus encourages the view that where the Holy Spirit is most clearly at work, there are little or no material elements involved. If the Holy Spirit operates without benefit of the material, then it is assumed that the inner experience of the person is a more pure avenue for the Holy Spirit to take than any experience involving the material world would be. As a result, persons who have had ecstatic personal experiences often believe that they are more spiritual and closer to God than those whose experience of God is mediated primarily through the everyday experiences of life.

This belief has one obvious flaw in logic. The inner experience of a person is not, in fact, any less material than is eating, drinking, or being involved in the world's affairs. Our inner religious experience must occur within and through our bodily structures— our brain cells, nervous systems, etc. If, therefore, the Holy Spirit only operates in nonmaterial ways, our only hope of experiencing the Holy Spirit would be to escape totally from this life and world.

More important, however, than this flaw in logic is the failure to understand the biblical God. From the beginning to the end of Scripture, God is involved with the material world. In the beginning God creates the material world and pronounces it good. God is revealed through the historical events of the material world. God calls people to serve in the material world by being merciful to widows and orphans, feeding the hungry, clothing the naked, and giving a drink of water in Jesus' name. In the sacraments the materials of bread, wine, and water become part of the worship of God.

The center of revelation for Christianity is in the human person of Jesus Christ who lived a human life, eating, drinking, growing weary, and who died a human death. If we believe in the Trinity and not in three gods, then we must assume that the same God who spoke in Christ is speaking as the Holy Spirit. That being so, we have no reason for assuming that the Holy Spirit will shun material means of communication. As God spoke to us in the human Jesus, so the Holy Spirit continues to speak to us through the events of daily life.

On the other hand, we cannot ignore the reality or importance of the inner personal experience of Christians. It would be strange indeed if the Holy Spirit could operate through the events of daily life but was helpless to speak within the inner life of a person. Those liberation theologies that see the socioeconomic experience of a person as the sole determining factor in life have fallen prey to an uncritical acceptance of certain forms of Marxism. Without denying that the socioeconomic context influences all experiences of a person, there is ample evidence in history that inner personal experience can motivate a person to swim against the stream of her or his class, race, or sex.

The basic form of revelation in the Bible is through the events of history as interpreted by a prophet. When the prophets made their claim, "Thus says the Lord," they were always interpreting the act of God within some historical event. Without the historical event there was no revelation. Nonetheless, their assurance that God was speaking depended on their inner personal awareness of God. For revelation to occur there was the necessity of both the external historical event and the internal personal illumination of the prophet who interpreted the event.

This form of biblical revelation comes out clearly in Matt. 16: 13-20. Jesus asked his disciples, "Who do you say that I am?" and Peter answered, "You are the Christ, the Son of the Living God." Jesus responded by telling Peter that he is blessed "For flesh and blood has not revealed this to you, but my Father who is in heaven." Here are the two elements necessary for revelation. Without Jesus, a living, breathing human being, there would be no revelation. And yet many who saw Jesus did not see him as the Christ. To see that, Peter needed to be illuminated by God.

Inasmuch as biblical revelation depends on both the historical events and the illumination of the prophetic interpreter, it is logical to conclude that Christian experience also will contain both elements. This being so, there is no reason for one Christian to look with disdain upon another Christian's experience. Those whose primary experience has been of an inner personal nature have no reason for boasting that they are more "spiritual" than others. And, by the same token, there is no basis for those who have found God most clearly in worldly events to boast that they are more "worldly" than others. In the twelfth and thirteenth chapters of 1 Corinthians Paul describes a host of the gifts of the Holy Spirit, culminating in the greatest gift, love. He reminds Christians that they do not all have the same gifts and this means that they do not all have the same experiences. But he emphasizes to them that this is no reason for one to boast over the other. All experiences and gifts play their part in the body of Christ, the church.

When we turn to the question of what place experience has as an authority for Christian life, we are asking how experience enters into the formation of beliefs and doctrines and how it provides assurance of salvation. We are asking how experience is related to the Scriptures which, traditionally, Protestants have claimed to be the ultimate authority for Christian life and doctrine. From our study it is apparent that there are several possible answers to these questions.

For some, experience is regarded as self-authenticating, it needs no other confirmation and it thus serves as a final authority for belief and theology. The God is dead theologians had experienced the death of God and this experience became the basis for their theology. Some of these theologians were modest in their claim about the authority of their experience. They did not assert that it was a final proof that God was, in fact, dead. But until they had further experience to change their minds, this experience had to be the basis for their theologizing. On the other hand, people who believe that they have experienced God speaking to them often believe that this is an authority that cannot be challenged by any merely mortal argument. In some cases, for example some of the radicals in Luther's time, such experiences take priority over the Scriptures themselves. Often when people have undergone particularly ecstatic experiences, such as being born again or speaking in tongues, the presence or absence of such experiences in other people becomes their criterion for deciding who is and who is not truly Christian.

There can be no question but that the conviction of certainty which comes from experience is very persuasive to the person who has had the experience. But a host of problems arise, as we have seen. Frequently two or more self-authenticating experiences contradict each other. The God is dead theologian experiences God's death and the charismatic Christian experiences God's living presence. How do we evaluate their experiences? There seems to be no religious belief held that cannot be authenticated by someone's experience. If we are to choose among experiences, we must have something beyond experience by which we test the experiences.

Experience as self-authenticating is open, as Karl Barth demonstrated, to the charge of Feuerbach that theology is merely anthropology written large; human beings project their human experience onto a heavenly screen and call it God. Likewise, experience as self-authenticating is open to Luther's charge that it lacks any way of distinguishing the Holy Spirit from the unholy spirits. Because human beings are affected by sin in their total nature, even their experience of God can be and often is perverted by sin.

However important our experience in religion may be, it cannot be taken as self-authenticating. We need something beyond experience by which we can choose between experiential claims and distinguish between the spirits. It seems, therefore, that Protestants should follow Luther's lead and bring experience under the judgment of Scripture, the final authority for Protestant faith. Even so, we find that there are different ways of relating experience and the Scripture.

Some have said that experience is the means whereby we know that the Scriptures are an authority. Some of the liberal theologians took the position that we know that the Bible is inspired because it inspires us. However, this leaves the problem that if there are portions of Scripture which do not inspire us, then we have no reason to believe that they are inspired. The end result of this position is that experience stands in judgment over the Scriptures. This position, therefore, has not really moved from the position of experience as self-authenticating and hence has all of the problems of that position.

Another approach is to argue that the Scriptures cannot be understood properly until the reader has had the proper experiences. Paul said that the Jews had read their Scriptures with a veil over their eyes so that it was only with the coming of Christ that the real meaning of the Scriptures could be comprehended (2 Cor. 3:12-18). It is not unusual to hear this passage quoted to argue that only those who have experienced the born again experience can understand the Scriptures. Similarly, many of the liberation theologians argue that only those who have experienced poverty and oppression can understand what the Scriptures are really saying.

It is evident that even in the Reformation where the Scriptures alone were being proclaimed as the ultimate authority, it was recognized that not everyone finds the same truths in the Scriptures. Therefore, the Reformers affirmed that the Holy Spirit must enlighten the reader of the Scriptures. For example, in the Formula of Concord we read that that Holy Spirit "opens the intellect and the heart to understand the Scriptures and to heed the Word. . . ." [1] There are problems in seeing how this is to be interpreted. Is the action of the Holy Spirit in enlightening the reader to be identified with a particular inner experience or does the Holy Spirit enlighten us through a variety of experiences which enables us to perceive in Scripture what we had not perceived before?

There is a danger in this position if the Holy Spirit is identified with an inner experience. If having the inner experience is the prerequisite for understanding the Scripture correctly, will the Scripture be allowed to stand in judgment over experience? Will not the experience predetermine what the Scriptures will be allowed to say? Most of the differing groups at the time of the Reformation would have agreed with the Formula of Concord that the Holy Spirit opens the intellect and heart to understand the Scriptures and each group was certain that the Holy Spirit had so opened their hearts and intellect. And so each group found Scripture supporting its position. In many ways this approach is like that of the liberal position which says that the Bible is inspired because it inspires us. Here it is our feeling of being inspired by the Holy Spirit which tells us what the Bible is saying. As the liberal position fell back into that of experience as self-authenticating, so this position is continually in danger of doing the same.

The Reformers themselves went beyond the view that it is a particular inner experience which enables us to understand Scripture correctly. They came to see that experience may provide a hermeneutic or principle of interpretation by which we read Scripture. This is obviously what happened in the case of Luther. His experience of anxiety and hopelessness that was overcome with his discovery of "The just shall live by faith" led him to see justification as the basic principle for interpreting Scripture. Similarly, liberation theologies believe that certain social experiences provide a hermeneutic that enables us to see the centrality of liberation in the Scriptures.

This position goes beyond the first three that we have examined. It is able to grant an authority to Scripture over and above all experience. A means of interpretation is justified only to the degree that it can facilitate the understanding of Scripture. Even though a person may have come to see a particular hermeneutical principal through experience, that person must be able to demonstrate to others that the hermeneutic fits the Scripture and is found in Scripture. Luther's information lasted because he was able to persuade others that the centrality of justification was a means of interpretation that unlocked the Scripture. It overcame the apparent contradictions in Scripture of law and gospel, God's love and wrath; it harmonized the two testaments, and in many other ways enabled the Scriptures to speak harmoniously to the reader.

In the same way, although the experience of the liberation theologians led them to see liberation as a key theme by which the Bible needs to be interpreted, they are able to demonstrate to others that the Bible itself justifies the centrality of salvation as liberation. Those who have not had the same experience are able to see that, in fact, the Bible does have a special concern for the liberation of the poor and the oppressed. In short, when experience provides a hermeneutical principle, it does not ask others to look at the experience of the person as such; it does not claim that the experience is self-authenticating. It says that this principle of interpretation can be validated by studying the Scriptures.

The followers of both Luther and Calvin formed "confessional" churches. That is, these churches had statements of faith which they confessed as the truth. In no way did these churches intend these confessions to take the place of Scripture or to stand above the Scriptures. The confessions always affirmed that the Scriptures alone are the final authority for faith and doctrine. The confessions were intended to be guides to the interpretation of Scriptures. They were affirmed because they were believed to be in harmony with Scripture and, by pointing to the central themes of Scripture, they could illuminate the understanding of Scripture.

Experience providing a hermeneutical principle which has to be justified by its ability to interpret Scripture has avoided many of the problems involved in the view of experience as self-authenticating. But, obviously, it has not avoided all of them. If someone fished a lake with a net whose holes were two inches in circumference and then used the catch to prove that there were no fish in the lake smaller than two inches in circumference, we would not be impressed. In the same way any principle of interpretation with which we approach the Scriptures (or any other written work) can operate like a net. It catches only those items that it is built to catch. Our principle of interpretation has certain questions that it puts to Scripture and it is not likely to get answers to questions that it does not ask. A principle of interpretation is always in danger of prematurely harmonizing different parts of Scripture and hence missing important variations within it.

Because of the dangers involved in principles of interpretation, many Christians from the time of the Reformation have insisted that their churches should have no creeds or confessions of faith. Their only creed, they have affirmed, is the Bible itself. Such groups sometimes refer to themselves as "Bible-believing" Christians to distinguish themselves from those who, in their eyes, are really creed-or-confession-believing Christians. Such groups often argue that they have carried out more consistently and logically the Reformation theme of "the Scriptures alone" than have those Protestant churches that have confessions.

The problem with Bible-believing Christianity is that we have to interpret Scripture if it is to speak today. Even if we limit ourselves to quoting Scripture, the very fact that we choose a particular passage to quote in a given context indicates that we have interpreted this passage as being relevant to this context. The Scriptures are silent on many of the problems with which the contemporary church has to wrestle. This means that we have to take what the Scriptures do say, which we interpret as relevant to the problem in hand, and try to interpret how the

Scriptural point of view should be applied to our problem. But, if we do have to interpret the Scriptures, ought we not to have some consistent principle of interpretation? If we do not, are we not continually in danger of interpreting ad hoc to our own advantage and interest?

Earlier we pointed out that the movement of born again Christianity rests heavily on the passage in John 3:3. In this passage a leader of the Pharisees, Nicodemus, comes to Jesus secretly and is open to Jesus' teachings. He is told that it is necessary to be "born anew." When Nicodemus treats this with a killing literalism, Jesus goes on to say that "unless one is born of water and the Spirit, he cannot enter the kingdom of God." (John 3:5). The born again movement interprets this text as saying that one can only be a Christian if they have gone through a particular inner experience. This is not the only possible interpretation of this passage. With the reference to water along with the Spirit, it can be interpreted to mean that being baptized is being born again. In verse 8 Jesus likens the Spirit to the wind that blows where it will without our knowing from whence it comes or goes. This could be interpreted to mean that what brings a person to faith cannot be located or identified and this would rule out any particular experience the person may have had. In short, the passage has to be interpreted before it can be used to justify the born again experience of today. Nicodemus was not the only Jewish leader who came seeking instruction from Jesus. In Matt. 19:16-22 and Mark 10:17-22 we read about a rich man coming to Jesus to ask how he might attain eternal life. Having found that the man claimed to have kept all the commandments, Jesus said that he lacked one thing. "Go, sell what you have, and give it to the poor, and you will have treasure in heaven; and come, follow me" (Mark 10:21). When the man went away sorrowfully, Jesus commented that it was hard indeed for a rich man to enter the kingdom. In fact, he said, it is easier for a camel to get through the eye of a needle.

Many of those who refer to themselves as born again Christians are also Bible-believing Christians who say that they accept the Bible as their only creed. But it is obvious that they are interpreting selected parts of the Bible. The words of Jesus to Nicodemus are taken as a requirement to be applied to all who wish to be Christian and they are interpreted as meaning that a person must go through the ecstatic experience that is described by them as being born again. However, none of them to my knowledge has suggested that Jesus' statement to the rich young man—to sell all his property and give it to the poor—should be a requirement of the Christian life or even that this is a definition of what it means to be "born anew." We must ask why the one passage is seen as central for becoming a Christian and the other is made peripheral or ignored altogether? In both passages Jesus is speaking to a potential convert and telling the conditions required of that person to enter the kingdom of God. The conditions given to only one of these men are the conditions presented by the born again movement to potential converts today. Why?

Obviously the born again movement is not simply following the Bible, it is interpreting the Bible. Our purpose is not to agree or disagree with the interpretation, it is simply to note that some principle of interpretation is involved. If the interpretation is well thought out and formulated, then these Bible-believing Christians are no different than the confessional churches. Both have their principles of interpretation although one group has spelled them out more officially than the other. If the Bible believers do not have some accepted principle of interpretation, they are open to the charge that their personal preferences have led them to follow the one passage and ignore the other. They have found the idea of being born again per-

sonally attractive but they have not wanted to sell their possessions and give the proceeds to the poor.

We seem to have arrived at an impasse. Experience, taken as
self-authenticating, faces problems of differing experience and
is open to the suspicion of self-interest coloring the experience.
Experience providing a principle of interpretation for the Scripture escapes some of the problems but cannot assure us that we
have a correct or adequate principle of interpretation. On the
other hand, to turn to the Bible as an authority without a principle of interpretation is impossible because we have to interpret
the Bible if it is to speak to us today. All in all it seems better
to have made our principle of interpretation explicit so that we
are conscious of what we are doing, but it can bring no assurance that we are correctly interpreting the Bible. Our principle
of interpretation, based on our experience, may fail to hear much
that we ought to hear in the Scripture. It is an impasse, however,
that we should expect if Luther's analysis of sin is correct.

Luther saw that the total nature of human beings is distorted
and affected by sin. Against those who believed that human reason had been unaffected by the fall so that reason could demonstrate the existence of God and learn something of God's nature,
Luther argued that reason is tainted by sin so that the God our
reason discovers is the God we want to discover. Against those
who believed that in their inner experience of God, they heard
clearly and purely the voice of God, Luther warned that inner
experience is also corrupted with sin and the God we experience
is the God we want to experience. For these reasons, Luther held
to the principle of the Scriptures alone, we must check all of our
reason and experience by the clear word of God's revelation. But
we must carry Luther's analysis even further. Our attempt to
test our reason and experience by Scripture requires us to interpret the Scripture, and our interpretations are always tainted by
sin. We end with the interpretation we want to find. Even if

we grant the premise that the Scriptures are the inerrant words of God, when we try to interpret those words, sin blurs our understanding.

When Christians are divided from each other by their experience and beliefs, it is not unusual to find that all are in agreement with Luther—they must test their experience and beliefs by the Scripture. And yet when they do, they find, to their satisfaction, that the Bible supports each of their particular conclusions. Charismatics who have had the experience of speaking in tongues find that the Bible blesses and promotes speaking in tongues. Those who find speaking in tongues to be repugnant find that the Bible disparages such speaking. One group's experience finds that Christianity is solely a message of individual salvation, another group's experience leads them to find that Christianity is solely or primarily a matter of redeeming all of society. Each group demonstrates that the Bible supports its position. One group finds that the Bible prohibits the ordination of women and another group finds that the Bible requires it. One group finds that the Bible clearly prohibits all abortions and another group finds that, under appropriate conditions, abortion is permissable. One group finds in the Bible a clear prohibition of all homosexual activity and another group finds a clear call to accept homosexuals. We could go on with the list indefinitely. Logically it would appear that not all of these interpretations of the Bible can be correct although logically they may all be wrong. The conclusion seems clear that the interpretation of Scripture is as affected by sin and/or finiteness as are reason and experience.

As we have seen, Luther emphasized that we can never find salvation or assurance of salvation from looking to ourselves. We cannot find it in our works, our reason or our experience. And now we must add that we cannot find it by looking to our interpretation of Scripture. Luther's theology of the cross was based on his understanding that we are always unworthy before God.

As a result, our attempts to know and express God are inevitably frail human attempts that are infected by sin. This, in part, is why God is always hidden even in revelation. Human nature wants something that it can hold and control to give security and assurance. And so while we may be ready to confess a theology of the cross at many points, we always try to keep one point of triumphalism. We may be prepared to admit that God's revelation contradicts our expectations. But, in our search for security, we become triumphalist at some other point. In our experience, we claim, we have known God purely and clearly or in our biblical interpretation we have grasped God fully and completely. It is difficult indeed for human nature to quit looking at itself to find assurance.

We argued earlier that today is an age of emphasis upon inner experience because we live in a world of rapid change that threatens our cherished values. In such a time it is natural for people to turn inward to find the security and assurance that the outer world cannot provide. In such a time there is a great danger, as Luther found in his time, that people come to depend on their inner experiences as the basis for their salvation and security. When this happens people begin to thank God that they are not like their neighbors who have not had their experiences. The church is divided and torn asunder by unseemly battles over experience. In saying this, we do not forget that in other times and places (and for some in our time and place) the same results have come from people finding security in their works, their reason or their interpretation of Scripture.

When we look to ourselves to find the basis and assurance of our salvation, it leads to a self-righteousness that divides us from our neighbors. This is inevitable because, if we hope to find our assurance within ourselves, we need to see ourselves as somehow superior to others. Like the Pharisee in Jesus' parable, we have to build up our own good works and the easiest way to do that is to thank God that we have done more than someone else (Luke 18:9-14). Similarly, when we depend on experience or doctrine, we need to show the lack of experience in others or demonstrate their faulty doctrines. But self-righteousness is not the only result of looking at ourselves for assurance; there is also the continual danger of despair.

In an age that depended on its good works for salvation and assurance, Luther fell into despair because he could never be sure that his works were good enough. Perhaps, he feared, he needed to do more than he had done and always he knew that he was doing good works for the wrong reason. Similarly, in an age that has depended on its inner experience there is the threat of despair. Sometimes it takes the form of fearing that more experiences are needed. The person who has had the experience of being born again now wonders if there can be certainty of salvation until he or she has spoken in tongues. The person who has spoken in tongues now wonders whether other charismatic gifts may not be necessary. But even more threatening to the person who depends on inner experience, is the fact that such experiences have a way of coming and going. This age that has emphasized the inner feelings of salvation and assurance is producing more and more despairing people who have had ecstatic experience in the past but now, for a long time, have experienced nothing, and they fear that it means they either never were saved or that they have lost their salvation. And, of course, those who try to find their assurance in their interpretation of Scripture are ever in danger of falling into the despair that comes with doubt about the correctness of their interpretation.

It was when Luther fell into despair that he heard the good news that what he could not find by looking at himself had been given to him by God. Luther had not been able to justify himself by his good works, but God had justified him by grace. We have seen that Luther said that sin is "total" in the sense that every aspect of human life is affected by it. It is necessary, therefore, to see that justification is also total, it affects the whole of life. The sinner who has failed to do good works is justified. The heretic who has misinterpreted the Bible is justified. The person whose inner experience has no feeling of God is justified. The one who doubts is justified. In every case, what could not be found by looking to the self has been given by God's grace.

Justification by grace through faith means a radical relativization of human life. Because God forgives sinners, our human works are relativized. Knowing that we have been accepted by God despite our failure to be righteous, we can no longer thank God that we are not like the other sinners around us. Similarly, our experiences are relativized. Some may have had more ecstatic experiences than others but that is no reason for feeling superior. No one's experiences are good enough to depend on. Some may have interpreted the Bible more profoundly than others but none of us can depend for salvation on our interpretations. Paul brings out this relativism when he says, "For by grace you have been saved through faith; and this is not your own doing, it is the gift of God—not because of works, lest any man should boast" (Eph. 2:8-9). Thus, what we find in ourselves is not the basis of our place before God.

When Luther came to understand justification by grace, he came to see good works in a new light. They were not the prerequisites of salvation, they were the means whereby we could express our love to God and our gratitude for what God has done for us. Because one has been freed from the anxious concern to save oneself by works, one could perform works more freely without continually worrying if they were proper, correctly motivated and so on. More important, one dared to be honest with oneself and to confess the shortcomings in one's works. This in turn could lead to a true repentance through which one might change one's works and the ways of doing them.

The same principles apply to experience. When we come to see that our relationship to God does not depend on what we have experienced, we are freed from anxious concern. We can be thankful for the experiences in which we have come to know God, but we no longer need to claim that our experiences are better than someone else's. Furthermore, because we no longer feel dependent on our experiences for salvation, we dare to look critically at them. We can ask if they come from the Holy Spirit or from unholy spirits. We can admit that our self-interest has colored what we experience. In such a condition we may be able to test the spirits as Scripture calls us to do.

The same principle also applies to our interpretation of the Bible. Confessing that our salvation does not depend on it, we can turn a critical eye on it. We do not have to claim that we alone are correct in our interpretation. We dare to accept the claim of liberation theology that our experience in our socioeconomic class has created our particular ideological interpretation of Scripture. We have interpreted the Bible so as to protect our social interests. And, since we can admit this inadequacy in our interpretation without fearing for our salvation, we are freed to look anew at the Bible and to see if the experiences of others may help us to find that in the Bible which we have not found before.

The point that we are making is illustrated well by the spiritual autobiography of C. S. Lewis. He calls his autobiography *Surprised By Joy* because he was brought to Christian faith through an ecstatic inner experience which occurred from time to time. This experience, which he found defied description, he simply called "joy." At the end of his life's story Lewis asks what about the place of joy in his present life. He says, "To tell you the truth, the subject has lost nearly all interest for me since I became a Christian." [2] It is not, he says, that the experience no longer occurs, it just does not seem so important to him. At the beginning the inner experience served as a pointer to God who was "other and outer." So long as God remained in doubt, the pointer naturally loomed large in his thoughts. The inner experience of joy had been like a signpost. When we are lost a signpost is a great matter, it points us to the right direction. But when the right road has been found and signposts are passed every few miles, little attention is paid to them, says Lewis.

What Lewis is pointing out here is that the Christian life cannot be lived by looking at the self or its experiences. Although inner experience may have played an important role in bringing us to faith, mature faith must cease being preoccupied with the self, and must look outside the self for its assurance. It is when we find our assurance beyond ourselves that we have the confidence that allows us to look at the self, its experience, its works, and its interpretation of the Bible, and to put all of them into the proper perspective. We dare to be critical of the self's attainments precisely because our assurance no longer rests there.

This is an age that emphasizes inner experience. As such it provides neither more nor less of an opportunity for Christian faith than other ages. It is neither more nor less a danger or a temptation to us than any other age. In all ages faith may arise from hearing the good news that God accepts us as we are. In all ages we are tempted to look at ourselves both for our salvation and our assurance. In different ages, with different emphasis, the form of the dangers and temptations vary. In the sixties we were tempted to believe that our good works were soon to save us and society. In the seventies we were tempted to think that because we had turned inward we were more spiritual and a great religious revival was at hand. Who knows what our temptations will be in the eighties? In all ages we need to remember "Let him who boasts, boast of the Lord. For it is not the man who commends himself that is accepted, but the man whom the Lord commends" (2 Cor. 10:17-18).

Notes

Chapter One—An Age of Experience.

1. Martin Marty. *The Search for a Usable Future*. Harper and Row, 1969, p. 32.
2. William Hamilton. "The New Optimist from Prufrock to Ringo" published in Thomas J.J. Altizer and William Hamilton, *The Death of God*, Bobbs-Merril, 1966. p. 158.
3. See William Hamilton's, "Beguiling Unfreedom," *The Christian Century*, Vol. LXXXVII, no. 39, Sept. 30, 1970, p. 1158.
4. Charles Reich, *The Greening of America*, Random House, 1970, p. 373
5. See Jacques Ellul, *The Technological Society*, Vintage Books, 1964 and Herbert Marcuse, *One Dimensional Man*, Beacon, 1964.
6. Theodore Roszak, *The Making of a Counter Culture*, Anchor Books, Doubleday, 1969, p. 205.
7. Theodore Roszak, *Where the Wasteland Ends*. Anchor Books, Doubleday, 1973, p. xv.
8. Ibid., p. 215.
9. e.g. see Alvin Toffler, *Future Shock*, Random House, 1970.
10. Ibid., p. 11.

Chapter Two—Experience, Knowledge, and Religious Experience

1. Friedrich Schleiermacher, *On Religion: Speeches to Its Cultured Despisers*, translated by John Oman, Harper, 1958, p. 15.
2. See Rudolf Otto, *The Iea of the Holy*, translated by John W. Harvey, Oxford, 1928.
3. Roger Nostbakken, "A Study-Report on the Charismatic Renewal Movement." A document circulated among the congregations and pastors of the Evangelical Lutheran Church of Canada.

4. Larry Christenson, *Speaking in Tongues,* Dimension Books, 1968, p. 130.

5. Colin W. Williams, *John Wesley's Theology Today.* Abingdon, 1960. p. 33.

6. Ibid., p. 34.

7. See John P. Kildahl, *The Psychology of Speaking in Tongues,* Harper and Row, 1972, pp. 40, 50, 54 and chapter 7.

8. William Hamilton, "A Funny Thing Happened on the Way to the Library." *The Christian Century,* April 12, 1967, Vol. LXXXIV, No. 15, pp. 469-70.

9. Hamilton, William, *On Taking God Out of the Dictionary,* 1974, p. 6.

Chapter Three—Luther and Religious Experience

1. Harry Loewen, *Luther and the Radicals,* Wilfred Laurier University Press, 1974.

2. Ibid., p. 9.

3. Bengt R. Hoffman, *Luther and the Mystics,* Augsburg Publishing House, 1976, p. 131.

4. Loewen, p. 51.

5. Quoted by Loewen, pp. 34-35.

6. Ibid., p. 111.

7. See Martin Luther, "Prefaces to the New Testament," *Luther's Works,* Vol. 35, p. 362. (Please note that, unless otherwise indicated, references to and quotations from Luther are from the English translation edited by Jaroslav Pelikan (vols. 1-30) and Helmut Lehman (vols. 31-55), published by Concordia Publishing House and Fortress Press.

8. *Luther's Works,* Vol. 35, p. 236.

9. *Luther's Works,* Vol. 19, p. 4.

10. *Luther's Works,* Vol. 40, p. 86.

11. *Luther's Works,* Vol. 35, p. 274.

12. Quoted by Reinhold Niebuhr, *The Nature and Destiny of Man,* Vol. 11, Charles Scribner's Sons, 1945, p. 170.

Chapter Four—Faith and Experience in Luther

1. Quoted by Martin Luther, *Luther's Works,* Vol. 40, p. 206.

2. Ibid., p. 207.

3. See Philip Watson, *Let God Be God,* The Epworth Press, 1947, chapter 11.

4. Ibid., p. 42.

5. Martin Luther, *Luther's Works,* Vol. 40, p. 241.

6. See Ian D. Kinston Siggins, *Martin Luther's Doctrine of Christ,* Yale University Press, 1970, pp. 147-148.

7. Luther, "Concerning Rebaptism, *Luther's Works,* Vol. 40, p. 243.

8. Ibid., p. 241.

9. Ibid., p. 239.

10. Ibid., p. 240.

11. Ibid., p. 246.

12. See for example Roland Bainton, *Here I stand*, Abingdon-Cokesbury, 1940, chapter 21.

13. *Luther's Works*, Vol. 40, pp. 248-249.

14. Karl Holl, *What Did Luther Understand by Religion?*, Fortress Press, 1977, p. 75.

15. Quoted by Holl, Ibid., p. 82.

16. Quoted by Philip Watson, *Let God Be God*, p. 167.

17. Martin Luther, *Large Catechism* in Theodore G. Tappert, The Book of Concord, Muhlenberg Press, p. 416.

Chapter Five—Luther's Theology of the Cross and Experience

1. *Luther's Works*, Vol. 31, p. 53.

2. Ian D. Kingston Siggins, *Martin Luther's Doctrine of Christ*, p. 42. See also *Luther's Works*, Vol. 24, p. 79.

3. See for example *Luther's Works*, vol. 22, p. 241.

4. Ian D. Kingston Siggins, *Martin Luther's Doctrine of Christ*, p. 35

5. *Luther's Works*, Vol. 22, pp. 492-493.

6. Ibid., p. 465.

7. Ibid., pp. 361-362.

8. Ibid., p. 189.

9. *Luther's Works*, Vol. 24, p. 217.

10. Ibid., p. 228.

11. Ibid., p. 231.

12. *Luther's Works*, Vol. 25, pp. 364-365.

13. Paul Althaus, *The Theology of Martin Luther*, translated by Robert C. Schultz, Fortress Press, 1966, p. 27.

14. *Luther's Works*, Vol. 40, p. 83.

15. Ibid., p. 146.

16. Ibid., p. 147.

17. *Luther's Works*, Vol. 24, p. 149.

18. Ibid., p. 151.

19. Ibid., p. 46.

20. Ibid., p. 67.

21. Ibid., p. 145.

22. Ibid., p. 420.

23. Ibid., p. 152.

24. Ibid., p. 362.

25. *Luther's Works*, Vol. 37, p. 219.

26. *Luther's Works*, Vol. 40, p. 203.

27. *Luther's Works*, Vol. 37, p. 92.

28. *Luther's Works*, Vol. 40, p. 187.

29. *Luther's Works*, Vol. 24, p. 231.

30. Ibid., p. 232.

31. *Luther's Works*, Vol. 24, p. 261.
32. *Luther's Works*, Vol. 37, p. 95.

Chapter Six—Experience and Liberation Theology

1. Martin E. Marty and Dean G. Peerman, *New Theology*, no. 9, Macmillan, 1972, p. 9.
2. James H. Cone, *Black Theology And Black Power*, Seabury, 1969, p. 31.
3. Ibid., p. 32.
4. Ibid., p. 36.
5. Ibid., p. 38.
6. Ibid., p. 85.
7. Ibid., p. 93.
8. Ibid., p. 97.
9. Alfredo Fierro, *The Militant Gospel*, translated by John Drury, Orbis, 1977, p. 244.
10. Dorothee Soelle, *Political Theology*, translated by John Shelley, Fortress, 1974, p. 49.
11. Phyllis Trible, *God and the Rhetoric of Sexuality*, Fortress, 1978, p. 4.
12. Ibid., p. 22.
13. Ibid., p. 56.
14. James H. Cone, *A Black Theology of Liberation*, Lippincott, 1970, pp. 23-24.

Chapter Seven—Particularism and Universalism in the Bible

1. Theodore G. Tappert, translator and editor, *The Book of Concord*, Muhlenberg, 1959, p. 464.
2. Ibid., p. 465.
3. Ibid., p. 90.
4. F. J. Taylor, "Redeem" in Alan Richardson (editor) *A Theological Word of The Bible*, Macmillan, 1951, p. 186.
5. Marty and Peerman, *New Theology*, no. 9, p. 13.

Chapter Eight—Conclusion

1. Tappert, *The Book of Concord*, p. 526.
2. C. S. Lewis, *Surprised By Joy*, Harcourt, Brace, 1955, p. 238.